THE POWER OF SELF DISCIPLINE

A Daily Beginner's Guide To Building Spartan Mental Toughness Even In Difficult Times.

Skyrocket Productivity and Achieve Your Success Goals By Resisting Temptation

POSITIVITY FOCUDED TEAM

Table of contents

Introduction

According to author M.R. Kopmeyer, "Self-discipline is the ability to make yourself do what you should do when you should do it, whether you feel like it or not."

No matter where you are at in life, you should hold yourself to a system that checks your excesses and keeps you in line.

"I don't just feel like it" has always been the major reason for procrastination. But if we keep waiting until we "feel like it" to come to action, we're in trouble.

Self-discipline can be explained in different ways. It could mean endurance, restraint, thinking before acting, perseverance, or carrying out your plans and decisions despite obstacles, hardships, or inconvenience. Self-discipline could mean self-control, too. This simply means avoiding unhealthy excesses which may have negative repercussions.

Whatever definition you fancy, one thing stands out about self-discipline: that innate ability to forgo instant pleasure and gratification in favor of more satisfying results or greater gain, even though it takes time and effort.

I have found that the term self-discipline carries a feeling of dread in many people. They see it as resistance and discomfort—something difficult to reach, nasty, requiring a great deal of sacrifice and effort. But this is quite the opposite. You can attain and exercise without having to undergo immense suffering.

Contrary to popular belief, real self-discipline is never punishing or restrictive of your lifestyle. It does not mean living like a monk or being narrow-minded. The truth is that self-discipline comes from a place of staying power and inner strength needed to manage life's everyday affairs while reaching your life goals.

By adopting a spirit of self-discipline, I have been able to overcome indecisiveness, procrastination, and laziness, which used to be the major challenges I faced. I saw myself taking bold actions and persevering with them, even though those actions seem demanding and unpleasant. I saw myself applying moderation in things I do. In the process, I became more considerate, understanding, tolerant and patient. For someone like me who was prone to bend easily to external influence and pressure, I began to take more control of my life. I saw myself not just setting goals but taking concrete steps to reach them. I became more punctual, putting more time and effort into the most important things in my life. I was exercising regularly, avoiding alcohol and drugs, stopped procrastinating and began to save for retirement.

Self-discipline comes with mastering your thoughts. By controlling what you think, you can control how you act. It comes with doing things when you don't want to. It comes with being free from weakness and laziness, being free from doubt and fear, and being from the demands and expectations of others.

Understand that the path to success is filled with a myriad of challenges. Getting there won't be easy. But if you can harness self-discipline (persistence + perseverance), like how I will show you in this book, you will rise above whatever problem and then live a happy and satisfied life.

Asides loss and failure in life, a lack of self-discipline can cause health and relationship problems. A lack of self-discipline can even be traced to addictions and eating disorders.

Chapter 1. What Is Self-Discipline?

Have you ever sat down and thought to yourself that you wish you could be more productive? Maybe you had just wasted another day, having had plans for all sorts of errands to get ahead on your work so you would not have to rush to get your project in on time, but instead of being successful about getting that project finished up, you wasted your time playing that new video game that you had been waiting months for. You had fun while you were playing it, but when you went to save the game and saw your time played, you realized that you had wasted hours of your time. Instead of being productive, you sat in front of a screen and played games. And you felt bad about it.

Maybe it was not video games for you. You may have been dedicated to losing some weight for your wedding to slip into that perfect dress but found that resisting the pumpkin pie and extra stuffing and green bean casserole during the holidays was too rough. Instead of abstaining or just having a small portion, you chose to live by the motto that calories do not count during the holiday season, and instead of losing any weight, you were dismayed to find that you actually put on five pounds instead of losing them.

No matter what your vice is, you may find that you regularly struggle to fight it off. You may procrastinate too much, fail to meet deadlines, or just generally fail to be productive and healthy. This is problematic, of course—you need to be healthy, not only for you but those who depend on you as well, such as your children if you have them. As discouraging as it can be when you realized that you had wasted yet another day or you have failed to lose that weight that you knew you needed to if you wanted to fit into that dress, you do not have to live with that sort of failure looming over you forever. Instead of falling into hopelessness, what if you took the energy that you spent worrying and chose to learn how to fix the problem once and for all?

Self-Discipline

Self-discipline is a skillset and also a lifestyle—you can have self-discipline skills but not necessarily be self-disciplined if you fail to use them on a regular basis. Not only must you learn the skills necessary, but you must also make sure that you are able to live that lifestyle as well. The entire purpose of self-discipline is to make the right decision, no matter whether it means you do not get that instant gratification that you were craving. When you are self-disciplined, you are able to get past that. You can see that brownie sitting on the corner and remind yourself that you have already had your treat for the day and that the brownie is out of the question, and then move on with your life as if nothing has happened.

Self-discipline can appear in many different forms that you may not realize. It can be perseverance—despite the challenge that you are facing, you can choose to keep going and keep trying, despite the exhaustion and despite the lack of motivation, you have to continue. It can be restraint—you can tell yourself that you will not be making a choice that may be enjoyable short-term, but you know will not be worth it long-term. It can be following your plan to a T instead of floundering between doing and not doing whatever your plan was until you are out of time anyway. It can be pushing past the hardships that whatever is required will cause and finishing the job, no matter what the cost or effort necessary.

Self-Discipline in Your Life

When you are self-disciplined, you are controlled. You are able to avoid negative consequences simply by knowing how to resist the temptation you feel that tries to convince you to do something. It is not the restrictive life of rejecting everything enjoyable that you may be thinking of—instead, it is an ability to balance your own goals and aspirations with what you really must do in order to see those results at the end of the day. You are able to enjoy yourself while not erring on the side of being lazy or greedy. Think of it as an exercise in moderation—when you are self-disciplined. You can live by that moderation without falling into the trap of eating or drinking in excess.

This lifestyle that you are living when you are self-disciplined is healthier, then. It is one with motivation, with drive, and with a clear idea of what you want to achieve and why. This is why self-discipline is so crucial, especially in today's world, where you dozens of ways in which you can satisfy yourself with instant gratification. Especially if you live in a major metro area, you may find that you have access to anything you may want within hours or days with delivery options available now. You do not have to leave the hope of buying anything—it can all be delivered straight to you. You do not have to go outside to make friends—you can do it online. You can even date online to find romantic partners without ever having to try to put in the effort to get to know the other person to see if you may be compatible—instead, you simply take a quiz, make a profile, and wait for computer algorithms to match you with other people that you may be compatible with.

In a world of being able to get anything and everything instantly without having to work for it or find it elsewhere, you have little in life that forces you to learn to be self-disciplined. Not much actually requires effort to become satisfied anymore. You do not have to hunt to survive, nor do you have to garden and forage. All you have to do is go to the store to buy something. If you have children, you can pay someone to come and take care of them for you. Essentially, these days, almost anything that required self-discipline before can be achieved with money.

Of course, you may be thinking of that old adage that money does not buy happiness, and that is exactly where self-discipline comes in. It is hard to feel satisfied and enjoyment in life when you are simply getting by with no effort. It is tough to feel like you are happy with yourself when you do not have to work to live. Life becomes boring and tedious, and you become unmotivated. Self-discipline can help you regain that motivation that you may have lost long ago and rekindled it into something powerful and helpful for you. Self-motivation can help you bring back the joy in your life that you may feel is lacking.

The Benefits of Self-Discipline

Now, you may be wondering what self-discipline can bring into your life. However, the better question may instead be to ask what it cannot do for your life. There are so many benefits of being self-disciplined, and you would see it in every aspect of your life if you were to develop it. All you need to do is try and stick to it, and you can find that it is entirely life changing.

When you have self-discipline in your life, you are able to do almost anything. You can overcome an addiction. You can learn a new skill. You can eliminate unhealthy or dangerous habits. You can bring more positivity into your life simply by changing your approach to your life.

Self-discipline helps you build character

Now, this may seem a bit too cliché to include, but it is an important point to keep in mind. You can be that person that you hope and aspire to be—that person that you want to be is your character. However, your character is constantly being undermined by emotions and the impulses that come along with your emotions. This means then that your emotions are actively sabotaging you—when you are emotional, you are unable to think or act in a rational way. This is problematic for you—you are likely to do things that you would otherwise wish you would not. If you are emotional, you may get labels that are not true to your character, such as vindictive or angry. Those around you will see you as angry or vindictive, and the only way to really fix that is to change your actions to match the person that you are on the inside. With self-discipline, you can control those impulses, ensuring that they do not control you instead, and you are able to make sure that you make decisions based on rationality instead of emotionality.

Self-discipline helps develop willpower

Stop and consider what your vice is for a moment—what is that one thing that you struggle to say no to? Is it candy? Wine? Your phone? Going out with friends? No matter what it is, you may find that sometimes, that vice can be detrimental to your goals, and you would be better off refraining. This does not mean that you can never have that glass of wine or let loose and have a few. This does not mean that you must cut out all processed sugar and hop on the Keto diet. However, you do need to be able to resist when partaking would be harmful. For example, you would obviously need to turn down that glass of wine if you are expected to drive or if you are at work. You would need to be able to cut out that sugar intake if you were ever pregnant and happened to be diagnosed with gestational diabetes. There are plenty of instances in which you need to be able to resist your temptations for the better good, and with self-discipline, you are able to finally achieve that.

As you develop your self-discipline abilities, you are able to resist these temptations. You are able to tell yourself that you do not have to give in and have that drink or that cookie because the short-term satisfaction is not worth the long-term harm that will come from giving in. You can see that partaking would be detrimental to your goals and what is in everyone's best interest, and you are able to stick to your goal.

Self-discipline is an indicator of successfulness

Let's face it—goals are not easy to achieve, especially if they are legitimately stretch goals for you. If you have set a good goal for yourself, you have some significant work that you need to do, and that work can be difficult to actually follow through on. Especially if you are presented with the choice to either follow through with your goal or do something that is bound to be much more enjoyable, it can be easy to slip through the cracks and give in to that temptation. This is where self-discipline helps to predict successfulness.

Think about what goes into actually achieving a goal for a moment—you must be able to not only create a plan for yourself, you must also be able to have the attitude to actually follow the plan. They are challenging and difficult to achieve but doing so only allows for further personal growth. As you develop your self-discipline, you develop the kind of goal-achieving attitude that will take you far in life. With it, you can ensure that you are able to meet your deadlines. You will be able to achieve your goals, even when it is inconvenient. This determination that it takes to keep pushing through to achieve your goal, even when you know that you would rather not achieve it in the first place, is enough to help push you toward being successful in general.

Of course, self-discipline is not a guarantee of success, but it is a skill that will help you reach it. To be successful, you need to know how to roll with the punches, how to make sure that you will continue fighting for what you want or need even when you know it is difficult, or you feel like fighting for that goal is not worth it. It will help you grow as an individual, and in growing, you will develop skills that will take you further in life than you may have ever anticipated being able to go.

Self-discipline creates a foundation for stronger relationships

Think for a moment about your current relationship or marriage if you have one. If you are not in a partnership of any kind, think of a relationship with your closest friend or family member. Stop and consider what things you value within that relationship. What makes that relationship and that individual important to you? Do you like who they are? Maybe you recognize that the other person is honorable or dependable. Those are not skills that come easily. Being honorable means that you have to do the right thing, even if it is detrimental to you to do so.

For example, imagine that you have lost your job and are facing eviction. Christmas is coming up, and you have children at home that you know are expecting Santa to come and bring them presents, and they need new winter gear. They do not know that just days before Christmas, they will likely be thrown out, and you have nowhere to go with them. You are walking down the road to the bus stop because you cannot afford gas for your car, and you happen to find a wallet on the ground. You pick it up and open it—you see a driver's license that was issued a few weeks ago so you can be pretty confident that the address is correct. Within that wallet, you also find a few thousand dollars in cash. Yes, that is much more money than most people are willing to carry, but it was sitting int hat wallet. What do you do?

The honorable individual would take the wallet to the address and try to give it back to the person that lost it, with all cash intact. It would be easy to take the money and pocket it without saying a word, but doing so would also mean that you are unlikely to be able to sleep at night, feeling guilty about taking what is probably someone's rent or car money, considering the amount.

When you develop self-discipline, you are able to develop those characteristics that make you seem more honorable and likable. You will be able to tell yourself that it is best to return all of the money intact, though keeping it would solve all of your problems for the next several months while you put together a long-term plan, and you will be able to follow through with that plan, no matter how much it hurts your heart to have that cash in hand and return it to someone else, knowing that you are facing homelessness without it.

Self-discipline then makes you a generally better person. You will act with integrity. You will be able to tell yourself that you have done the right thing, and that is enough for you.

Self-discipline makes you more even-tempered

Think about how easy it is to get offended about something. It does not take much to push someone over the edge, especially if they are someone who tends to err on the side of emotionality instead of rationality. However, this is something that you can learn to overcome. You do not have to be hotheaded or temperamental when you have self-discipline. In fact, you can intentionally learn how to overcome those negative feelings before they can pose a problem for you.

People with self-discipline know how to keep those strong emotions that may lead many people to act impulsively. When you learn this skill, you can tell yourself what is best for you is to remain calm and follow through. You are more confident as a direct result of that ability to remain calm, even when faced with adversity. You are able to be confident that you are doing the right thing, and with that confidence also comes calmness and security in your choice. You know that you are making a good decision, one that is morally correct, and that is enough to keep you calm.

Along with this even-tempered attitude comes the confidence that you have always tried your best, and with that, comes peace of mind. You can only ever be expected to do your best, as anything else is an impossibility. If you can honestly say that you have tried your best, then you have done everything that there is to be done, and that is good enough.

Lacking Self-Discipline

As important as self-discipline is, it is, unfortunately, not something that is innate within people. You are not born to be self-disciplined—you must learn to be self-disciplined. Learning to develop it can be difficult if you do not have the guidance necessary to figure out what to do or how to do it. If you find that you are not being guided through the process, it can be quite simple to just give up instead of attempting to pursue it.

Chapter 2. Why Be Self-Disciplined?

For a wholesome, happy, and productive life, you are going to need these three things: to love yourself (self-love), to be confident in yourself (self-confidence) and to be mentally tough. Discipline will help you gain them.

Self-Discipline is Self- Love

It can never be emphasized enough how much self-love matters for happiness and even productivity. Many ideas and tips about how to master self-love have been shared. However, the best of them all is mastering self-discipline, because to be disciplined is to love you. How, you may ask. Let me explain.

What does it mean to love yourself?

Self-love is not satisfying every one of your whims

In case you are wondering, self-love is not doing everything you want to do out of a whim to be happy in the moment. There are many things that feel really good, but they are not good for you. For instance, smoke a joint to feel good for a few minutes, eat fast food because it tastes great, have casual sex with every hot person you meet because it feels good or watch a TV show all day, hang out with some gang because they are fun etc. In the long run, this kind of stuff will destroy your life. This is not self-love, its self-destruction.

Self-love is doing things that are good for you in the long-term

Self-love means that you cherish yourself. It means that you do the things that are good for your mind and body. You do things that will make a better future for you. When you love yourself, you do not do things that may harm you now or in future, even if they seem to be fun at the moment. You care for yourself and do what you have to do for a better life now and in future.

Discipline Enables Self-Love

Self-discipline is self-regulation that helps you to have power over impulses and make you strong against your weaknesses. If you have something like a social media addiction, a disabling weakness in our generation today, you can win against it, make yourself put the devices away and get to attend to your tasks. If you are on a weight loss journey but French fries and chicken wings are your weakness, you are able to say no to the temptation to stick with your smoothies, vegetables and whole grains.

When you have discipline, you are able to get yourself to do things that are good for you even if they are hard or unpleasant. You see some things are very pleasant, but their pleasure is quite temporary while their consequences are painful. Those who do not have self-discipline will easily get carried away and suffer the consequences. However, if you are disciplined, you will be able to resist and make better choices that are good for you, even if it means missing out on the 'fun' and enduring quite unpleasant processes. If this isn't self-love, what is?

You cannot love yourself without mastering self-discipline

Self-Love Motto: "I love you so much that I can deny you pleasures that can harm you, because I want you to be happy tomorrow. For that I will endure the sacrifice today."

Discipline's motto: "To endure the pain of sacrifice now, so that you can enjoy the sweet fruits tomorrow"

They work together; Self-discipline is self-love. If you want to cultivate self-love, master self-discipline. That's how to love yourself and consequently, that's how you find peace and true happiness.

Self-Discipline and Self-Confidence

There is a connection between self-confidence and self-discipline. Let me explain.

It is gratifying when you take action on an idea and start to bring it to life or tackle something on your task list successfully. Achievement boosts confidence. When you achieve your objectives for the day, you feel proud of yourself. It goes a long way in raising your belief in self and self-esteem.

Consequently, you become more confident in your work and your ability to deliver. You need this confidence to succeed as it means you are no longer afraid that you will fail to deliver or screw up things; you know that you can do it. When you are this confident, you begin to seek more opportunities and take more chances at growing and improving yourself.

Achievement is driven by discipline

Nothing is achieved by mere chance or luck. Keeping in mind that the process to attain worthwhile achievements is not easy, it is almost impossible to do it if you lack discipline.

You need self-discipline and all its elements to achieve whatever you put your mind to. Each time you force yourself to do something that you ought to do, fighting the urge to give up, that is discipline at work. When you work and when you get it done (when you achieve) your confidence gets a boost.

Discipline begets achievement, which boosts confidence

Confidence is not automatic. For other people to have confidence in you, you have to prove yourself, right? It works the same way if you are to believe in you; you have to prove yourself to yourself. This is done by doing what you said you will do and achieving what you set your heart and mind on. I don't know anyone who liked themselves for being a looser who never get's anything done. But, I know many people who are proud of themselves for getting things done and delivering results.

Once you have self-confidence, there is nothing you cannot achieve. Discipline is the only force that can push you to such achievements.

Discipline gives you control, which boosts confidence

Being able to control yourself, your emotions and moods will help boost your confidence. You have greater belief in yourself when you are certain that factors such as emotions, moods or other people's influence cannot override you. Discipline gives you control over actions, reactions, and feelings. You will be more confident when you become the master and not a victim of these factors.

Discipline improves your self-image

How you see yourself has a lot to do with self-confidence. There is no way you can be confident with poor self-image. If you see yourself as unworthy, ugly or a loser, you will not be confident. However regardless of who you are or what you have done, if you know that you are in control and that you have the ability to change your life to become what you want, and that you can actually do it successfully, you start to see yourself through positive lens.

Self-discipline is the only guarantee that you can change, because in discipline, you do what you need to, no matter what. This assurance will boost your confidence and you can walk with your head high, even if your circumstance or conditions are not, as good as you want them to be – you know you can and will change them.

Therefore, if you want to be more confident, do not just hope or recite mantras, work on your self-discipline.

Self-Discipline will Help You Build Mental Toughness, which You Need to Thrive

Some people thrive in life, even when faced by tough circumstances and they achieve success almost in every area of their lives. On the other hand, another kind of people merely survives, and they live through life complaining and wishing that things would be better for them. They barely achieve anything.

According to experts, the main difference between the thriving and successful and the unsuccessful survivors is Mental Toughness.

What is mental toughness?

One definition defines it as the possession of psychological ability that allows one to 'perform at peak maximum effort and efficiency to deliver on the demands placed on them, especially when the demands are greatest or conditions become adverse'.

Otherwise known as mental fortitude, simply put, this is the ability to have a positive mental attitude, coping skills and the resilience to withstand and overcome challenges in life. They say that you should never expect life to be easy and without challenges; it is not tailor made for any particular person.

The only thing you can do to ensure that you thrive is to find a way to withstand and overcome the inevitable challenges. There is no better way to do this than to build mental toughness – to become mentally strong or as popularly know, 'grit.' Grit more than anything else plays a very important role in enabling you achieve your goals in all areas of your life.

Characteristics of mental toughness

Self- confidence

Determination

Composure

Self-control

Persistence

Leadership

Self-motivation

Focus

Positive energy

Calmness in the midst of 'storms'

This is what mental toughness will do for you:

It will sustain your courage and resolve even in the most difficult situations

Mental toughness is what makes soldiers. The rest of us run from war or any sort of danger. However, soldiers will advance towards it, with a strong belief that they will conquer. We may assume that they do it out of duty – partly maybe. However, no one would court and conquer danger and difficult situations merely out of duty. Duty will not give you courage to go forward, it will not help you cope with the challenges nor will it make you resilient and unbreakable under pressure. Duty is not enough to make anyone stay the course.

However, mental toughness will. That is what soldiers are majorly trained to build. They are put through tough and difficult test exercises, which stretch the limits of their physical, mental and emotional strengths. These tests are hard and unpleasant. Despite this, they are expected to complete them, with even more unpleasant consequences if anyone refused to do them.

A cadet has no option but to adjust their attitude, build resilience and prepare their mind and body to take it. There is something else that they have to get to successfully complete their course despite the challenges; you guessed it right, it is discipline that helps them build that mental toughness. Discipline here is a habit, to do what you have to do. It could be why they are collectively referred as 'The Disciplined Forces' – and why they go to war front, scenes of terror and worst possible situations to do what they have to do without cowering, even though it is as scary as hell.

It will lead you to success

All successful people have mental toughness. On the road to success in every sphere of life, you will be tested. A mentally tough person does not crumble under pressure. They thrive.

Unlike talent, grit is not inborn; it is not in anyone's DNA. That is why talent or ability does not guarantee success. You may be talented and perform well in normal circumstances, when you are feeling great and things are good. However, when things get out balance and challenges arise, you crush under pressure.

On the other hand, a person who has had to grow their abilities and has mastered mental toughness, pressure does not crumble them; it strengthens them. If the fight gets harder, they grow muscles to fight even harder. Like a soldier, there are no excuses or falling back when it gets tough. This person delivers results; such a person succeeds.

It takes discipline to build mental toughness

To change your mindset from being mentally weak to tough, you must apply discipline. You must purposefully decide that you are going to think in a way that empowers you and bury the self-defeating weak mentality. It takes a lot of discipline to actually make the change and stick with it.

Also, to grow mental toughness, you need to make a decision to be in control. Self-control is an element of discipline. It means that you do not let events, circumstance or people control what you do or how you react. You decide from a point of awareness what you do and how you react.

Grit requires resolve. You need to be decided to do something, whatever happens. The resolve to move forward ought to be stronger than the fears and doubts that never fail to creep in our minds. Self-discipline in itself is a resolve, as mentioned earlier, to do what you have to do; only a disciplined person can have such a strong resolve and not bend to pressure or influence.

Chapter 3. Self-Discipline Psychology

Special Forces Selection is designed to test the minds and bodies of potential operators. They realized a long time ago that the mind is their most important tool. This is why you too have to master your own psychology to reach your goals and take your life to the next level.

Self-Discipline is generally an act of will, so it is important to understand how the human mind works. This is done in order to convert understanding to a greater sense of self-control. Over millions of years, the human being has evolved an even more complex brain. Psychology, as a human endeavor, has shed some light into the mysteries of the mind, finally allowing us to see how things affect or motivate people and how our environment affects how we react to things that occur. We will look at four relevant things: the self-image, the locus of control, classical conditioning, and the psychology of motivation.

Self-Image

The way a man perceives himself affects how he reacts to the world. This is shaped by how he was raised, or the kind of people that have surrounded him. The environment he grew up in has shaped how he sees himself. There are men who have low self-esteem, and this makes them believe that they are unworthy of good things, or that they are incapable of achieving perfection.

On the other hand, there are others who have an inflated sense of self-worth, and they believe that they deserve everything without actually having to do much. These men, though they may seem powerful on the outside, are in fact hollow. Cracks on their tough shell will show an overwhelming insecurity that they have spent a lifetime hiding. If a man is on the quest to becoming a true alpha male he must be able to know the truth about himself and not give in to insecurity or the temptation to take the easy road by simply hiding under a facade.?

There can be no guarantee, however, that we will be able to understand ourselves immediately; and in fact, even psychology has not been able to get us a definite answer. But if the goal of the man is to become an alpha male, then he must be open to feedback. Negative feedback serves as a way for the man to take a detour from the path he has taken and improve himself. Focusing on negative feedback, however, won't do much good.

Negative feedback only works as a way to know if we are going the right way. However, the man must be able to discern whether or not the feedback comes from true and reliable sources--often, in the interest of politicking, people tend to lie about what they really think of you. Thus, the man must only accept feedback from the people he trusts to be brutally honest, such as a mentor or even enemies. Enemies have no interest in you and, by definition, hate you to the core. So, they will have no interest in sugar-coating anything. They will be absolutely, brutally honest.

It is wise to not to be too emotional about what they have to say and instead take it as a way to improve--not for them, but for yourself, the ideal you want to achieve, or the movement you are fighting for.

Locus of Control

A man on the path to self-improvement must find out whether he blames others for the things that happen to him or if he blames himself for what happens to him. If the man blames others all the time for everything that happens to him, it can be said that his locus of control is said to be external, which means that he lets go of his power to fate or "destiny". This is the weak man's approach, especially if he believes that he is unable to change anything that happens to him. He is weak-minded and weak-willed, and he thinks that whatever happens to him is because of random chance and other people or events. This is a lazy and weak approach to life.

On the other hand, a man whose locus of control is internal tends to see everything as his fault, and if this goes to the extreme, he ends up being too overwhelmed by what is happening to him and even to the world. He might blame himself about something that happened to someone totally unrelated to him. This is unrealistic. We go back to the topic of the self-image: the man must be able to have the right information about himself in order to act upon it.

It is important that the man can balance both loci of control, and so he must be able to take responsibility for what he does. Taking responsibility strengthens the ability to take bigger risks, and it allows the man to step outside of his comfort zone. In order to become a self-disciplined alpha male, the man must be able to push himself further and further, pushing the boundaries or his comfort zone until this zone disappears.

Classical Conditioning

To challenge the idea that psychology was an armchair pseudoscience, the behaviorist movement, which included the psychologist Ivan Pavlov, brought the scientific method into the field through experimentation. Pavlov was able to show the process of training and conditioning by measuring how much dogs salivated every time a bell is rung to signify food. After the experimenter rings the bell, he puts the food out. Soon, even when he does not bring out food, the mere ringing of the bell has been shown to make the dogs react as if to get ready for food. This is called conditioning, and another way to apply this concept is reward and punishment.

People and animals tend to stay from punishment, and they tend to look for rewards. So, rewards will make us keep doing what we were doing in order to get the pleasure of that reward. Punishments work the other way around, so the balance of both reward and punishment will effectively condition a person to a certain kind of action. Because we were born with the capacity to rule ourselves, we can consciously apply this method to ourselves in order to achieve the kind of action we want to learn. Ask yourself how much pain you will get if you don't take action. For example, how much pain will you get if you don't study for your exam? Maybe you will not graduate. Now think about the short-term pain of studying versus the long-term pain of not graduating. Now think of the reward or pleasure you will get if you do the study. You will graduate with a degree and be respected by others. So in this way you can trick yourself into doing things that you don't feel like doing.

Psychology of Motivation

When people are asked who will win between a lion and a man in an arena, most people answer the lion because it is more powerful, and it has evolved to be stronger than the man. Unless that man is the mythical Hercules, the lion will no doubt devour the man. However, this does not take into consideration the sort of evolution that humanity has gone through in the past millions of years. The human has evolved a more complex brain and the ability to innovate and create weapons. Thus, a fairer fight would be between a lion and a man armed with weapons?

Humans are more complex than animals, and the difference is evident in our desire to become greater than ourselves. This book is already a testament to that. Thus, in motivating a man to become better than himself, it is important that he knows what he is fighting for. He needs a goal, and a way to know whether or not he has achieved it. Not knowing what he is fighting for, even the hardened warrior will fail. A man with a purpose is unstoppable.?

Once the man has decided on his goal, he must begin to act. Success is being and doing what you want now; and that can only be achieved if you act immediately and act as if that success is already present now. Soon, even without thinking about it, the goal will have already been reached. It is also important, then, to trust in the process or habit through the continuous application of self-discipline.

Chapter 4. How Motivation Feeds Self-Discipline

Grow Your Knowledge

The initial step to cultivating your self-confidence is making sure that you acquire knowledge both in your private and professional undertakings. There is constantly that area for which you sense you lack in understanding and knowledge.

If you wish to have more self-confidence, then you need to show mastery in this field. You can broaden your understanding by taking online courses, participating in comparable conferences and occasions, along with reading books. The other thing that you can delight in while acquiring knowledge are tele classes, where you get to communicate and participate in discussions with your peers. This is going to go a long way in enhancing your degree of self-confidence.

Appreciate Smaller Wins

Unshakeable self-confidence originates from the capability to experience and celebrate little successes and victories. Consider this as providing prizes for using knowledge. Do you remember the part about micro-goals? Well, each time you attain a micro-goal, you reward yourself. Yes, they are not the supreme goal, yet they are little pieces that comprise the larger goal.

The prize does not need to be large. Even a basic pat on the back or only a sincere compliment from an associate is enough to improve your level of self-confidence. For that reason, make sure that you monitor each little accomplishment and enable yourself to experience it totally. By doing this, you are going to begin to feel your self-confidence growing every single day.

Believe in Something

Among the qualities I appreciate about confident individuals is that they believe in a supreme being. They think that the maker of the universe has a role for each living soul. Simply put, the reason why we are on the planet right now is to find and fulfill our more significant purpose.

They appear to have superb knowledge that when they follow the plan of the creator, attaining success is simply a matter of time. For that reason, if you really wish to accomplish success, you need to have faith that it is achievable. You must have undeviating confidence in your ability. When your faith is loaded with enthusiasm, then there is a high probability that you are going to follow your real purpose.

Cultivate A Firm Resolve

Within this life, it is natural that you are going to deal with obstacles and frustrations in the process. It is, for that reason, natural to feel mad and dissuaded. Nevertheless, you must see these problems as a chance for learning for something larger yet to take place in your future.

When you show faith in your capabilities, you are going to surpass discouragements and get a strong resolve. It is this resolve that is going to, consequently, help you conquer challenges. This is primarily since firm resolve is a real mark of perseverance at work. Instead of despairing, you are going to understand that without these difficulties, you would not have a growth mindset. Your mind must be concentrated on the desired result and not on obstructions. Rather than thinking about a thousand reasons why you can't, think about one reason why you can.

With time, you are going to see your talents turn into skills. It is just then that you are going to start to see what is genuinely possible, a measure of success guiding you forward with a lot of vitality and passion. It is this passion that is going to keep you ignited to keep scoring those little micro-goals.

Work With Professionals

Determine places where you have gaps in understanding which you wish to fill up. As soon as you do that, get assistance from experts that are going to assist you in acquiring more knowledge and experience. Understanding that you have professionals' support, you are going to be more confident when acting and deciding additionally. You can learn from professionals from books, blog sites, videos, phone calls, one-on-one meetings, workshops, and so on. The benefit of an expert coach is that they are going to assist you to stay accountable for each action you take in finishing your program.

Keep in mind that, if you desire self-confidence, then you need to draw in self-confidence. Yes, professionals are going to show you the way. However, they are not going to walk the road for you. You need to want to go through all challenges with your head held high your eyes on the reward. Ultimately, you are going to arrive there.

Visualize Your Confident Self

When you can view yourself as somebody confident, then self-confidence is going to end up being a characteristic that is simple and natural to demonstrate in reality. You begin to experience it directly. Take a minute to envision yourself having the self-confidence that you require in a particular scenario.

Picture how you would think and behave if you had the self-confidence you are after. Preferably, close your eyes and see yourself utilizing your mind's eye, acting with a lot of self-confidence and conviction. Keep that image in your mind, and you are going to understand that your vision is going to start taking root and coming true.

Believe That You Deserve Confidence

Did you understand that expectations are faith at work? At this moment, you have currently imagined yourself being self-assured and how you would feel after that. When you are self-confident, you are going to talk, act, and move surely and with a lot of passion as you pursue your objectives. This is when you understand that you have the sight, emotions, and actions of a self-confident individual. Simply put, you are going to be far better positioned to accomplish a lot more than you expected. When you expect to be confident, it comes to fruition.

Like we have currently said, self-confidence is not something that occurs overnight. You need to put these actionable suggestions into practice over months. Begin by jotting down ways in which you plan to use these actions. In this manner, you understand precisely how it would be like to act towards your goal. When you act upon them, you begin understanding significant improvements in your self-confidence, and quickly this equates to self-esteem, joy, happiness, and supreme success in life.

Only when you invest the necessary energy into your self-discipline will it function correctly, taking you to your desired destination.

Creating your motivation

One of the most vital energies that your self-discipline relies on is motivation. This is probably the single thing that keeps so many people from achieving the success that they so desperately desire. No amount of self-discipline can help you to achieve your goals in life unless you have the motivation needed to keep things moving along. In short, self-discipline without motivation is no different than an engine without gas.

Therefore, the first thing you need to do is to ensure that your goals actually belong to you and that they aren't ideas placed into your mind by someone else. Before you begin to plan and plot your way to a destination you need to decide that the destination is where you really want to go, if it isn't, you will face an uphill battle each and every step along the way. Time after time, you will struggle with the obstacles and pitfalls along the way to achieving your goal, without any real incentive to persevere. Regardless of whether you are pursuing a dream to please your parents, a spouse, or even social norms, it all boils down to the same scenario. If the dream doesn't come from your heart, you won't have the fire in your belly that drives, you to your success.

Once you have determined that your goal truly belongs to you, the next step is to discover the reason behind the goal. Every purpose has an underlying cause, something that makes a particular goal worth pursuing.

Alternatively, you might want to achieve a goal because of the lifestyle you believe it will offer you. No matter what your motivation is, the important thing is to discover it so that it can help fuel the self-discipline you need in order to achieve your dream.

Reward and punishment

Another way to establish motivation in your life is to create a system of reward and punishment. The idea of punishment for failure shouldn't be interpreted as causing yourself pain and suffering whenever you fall short, rather it is a matter of withholding certain pleasures from yourself when you engage in negative behavior. By withholding things that bring pleasure when you engage in negative behavior and indulging in them when you put forth your best efforts you will create a very real value system in your mind that will redefine how you see self-discipline.

One of the reasons why so many people never pursue a dream, or a meaningful goal is that they have an easy enough life without achieving their dreams. People can indulge in their favorite coffee drinks, fancy pastries, or any other number of tasty temptations any time, any day. This turns those things that would be rewarded into everyday items, removing their true value as well as the potential they have for helping you to succeed. By withholding such things from yourself when you go astray, you create a sense of punishment that you will want to avoid. Again, this isn't about creating pain in your life; rather, it is about encouraging you to steer clear of certain behaviors or activities.

Creating a competitive environment

Finally, there is the aspect of creating a competitive environment. What most people don't realize is that the energy in their mind is directly affected by the strength of their surroundings. Thus, the more time a person spends in a negative environment, the more negative their energies will become. The very same thing holds in terms of people. When a person surrounds themselves with negative people, their mindset will become harmful as a result. The solution is to create a competitive environment. This is what is meant by placing yourself in the right places and around the right people in order to bring out your best in terms of effort, talent, and overall self-discipline.

The first step to creating a competitive environment is to distinguish the difference between positive and negative situations clearly. Any place that encourages laziness, self-pity, negative thinking, and other such toxic energies is a place that you need to avoid. Such environments can include cheap bars where people go to drown their sorrows in alcohol and thus avoid facing their problems head-on. Basically, any place that attracts deadbeats, dropouts and those with low self-esteem are places you want to steer well clear of.

In addition to avoiding negative places and people, you must find positive situations and people to replace them with. Just as the negative energy from spiteful, lazy people can influence your power, so too can the positive energy from successful, highly motivated people.

Chapter 5. How To Develop Self-Discipline?

When we say that guy, for instance, is self-driven and disciplined, what does it mean? This statement is enough proof that mental strength and self-control link up and make individuals successful. Self-discipline can also be referred to as willpower. It is the ability to resist desires that are quite hard to say no to, but you get the ability to forgo them. Mental strength, on the other hand, is the capacity to deal neatly and effectively with negative pressure, thoughts, stressors, and challenges and come out as the best. Mental strength assists you in making a way through those obstacles irrespective of how challenging or against us. A combination of mental strength and self-control will give you the ability and confidence to make sure you make it through pleasures and desires and enjoy the rigidity on the other hand. A man in which both traits knitted together is highly perceived successful.

The Brain as a Control Unit

Being mentally strong is directly proportional to self-discipline. A mind is a great tool and device that has powers and capabilities, both positive and negative. The human brain can destroy or build. Always keep in mind that the choice is yours and for it to build or destroy, then it has to be well equipped and trained in that aspect. Whatever you feed your mind with is what it will radiate in exchange. By training your mind to be strong, it achieves brain muscle, and it becomes strong and capable of fighting whatever situation comes to its way. The power of the mind is valued so much. Even during job interviews, the questions thrown at you help describe the person you are, how you think, act, and answer the questions tells a lot about you.

Like bodybuilders go to the gym and lift weights to strengthen their muscles, so should you? Nonetheless, the brain's gym in this world is the day to day situations. They are the weights. To build brainpower, you need first to be someone who is positive and a believer. Live positively, and even if the world throws you negative things from them, find at least one positive, and it will stand out. If personal development is your goal, then mental strength is a great tool. To obtain the mental strength here is where self-discipline kicks in, you have to focus on healthy mental habits. To concentrate on the habits, you will require self-control, which will be a reminder that you are doing this to achieve that. With self-discipline, all will all in place, and the mental muscles will experience constant exercises.

Mental strength is not something that will be obtained overnight. You have to work hard for it and avoid habits that will affect the process. Practice virtues focus on yourself and believe in yourself in that nobody can put you down. The advantage of this combination of self-discipline and mental strength is that your self-worth will elevate, and you will feel good about yourself eventually.

Saying No to Temptations and Other Habits

Temptations are part and parcel of the life we live. It takes a strong mind and self-discipline to keep away some temptations. Temptations, however, come in different magnitudes and areas. Some temptations are easy to forego, but others seem like huge barriers ahead of us. It is a mindset though, what you perceive as impossible to avoid to you is a piece of cake to another person and the vice versa is also true to some extent. To expound better and understand this, let me use examples.

Early in the morning, some of us have a tendency to feel bad if woken up early. If the alarm is responsible, we have the great will to snooze it and continue sleeping, if it is someone else, then we feel the nagging effect, and we may even get angry and emotional at them. To overcome this, get the courage to wake up, leave the warm, comfortable bed, and face the happenings and schedules of the day, it requires a strong will and discipline. Practicing daily waking up and moving on will build the muscles of the mind and gain discipline. It is something that will take a while, but repeatedly doing the same will make you more focused on what lays ahead of you than what is in the bed.

Let us take another example of someone who is already married, has a job, and is successful. The only thing this person lacks is the ability and courage to say no to alcohol. His wife at home is constantly complaining, and some evening, they even get into arguments. This guy, however, is one of the good guys, but his friends are not that disciplined. After work, this guy lets name him Peter, will pass by a joint that is strategically situated on the route that he uses while going home, and it is a few meters from his working place. They will leave work in the evening, and his friends will ask him out for drinks. He doesn't want that because firstly he has a family and secondly, he is not willing to get drunk. Due to a lack of self-drive, he will accept the offer and promise to take only two beers. Peter ends up getting drunk by taking more than the two beers. He will go home, and the argument starts, and many issues will follow. If this cycle continues even if not on a daily basis, then it is a bad habit.

Advice to him would be that he focus on the keeping of bad friends and alcohol. This, however, cannot be achieved overnight. To become self-disciplined as well as gain the power of the mind, it will require him to practice wisdom and virtues so that he can turn down the offers of his friends without breaking the relationship and also without hurting their feelings or being afraid of hurting them. That's just a step towards a better direction, and he also has to make sure he has made a firm decision on avoiding alcohol since the club is just along the way to his home. He can find another route or face the situation and focus ahead.

Indicators of mental strength and self-discipline are lack of excuses and courage to say no to temptations that add no value to you. Mental toughness once acquired, will make you stop making excuses and will help you also focus ahead and avoid any attempt against achieving your set goals. Mental toughness, therefore, goes hand in hand with the ability to control one's desires. Practicing emotional intelligence and saying no to temptations and excuses repeatedly will increase and broaden your will power. You become stronger against these temptations, and you will face them head-on.

Self-awareness

The focus is on you; it has been proven that individuals that are able to attain mental toughness are well behaved and very successful. Your body health state also contributes to the progress of attaining mental toughness. You need a healthy body to facilitate the process of self-discipline and mental toughness. Feeding right and healthy foods will keep the body in good shape. A well-informed person will not forgo the need for a good healthy body statue. Nutrition will help provide the energy required by the body and brain in taking up the challenges and facilitate the process of change. The brain releases free radicals while working; the number of free radicals released is directly proportional to the activity of the brain. The food we take in, on the other hand, has elements that will bind to these radicals and eliminate them. The complex made by element and radical will exit the mind, and it will feel fresh again hence the need for good feeding habits.

By taking care of the body also involves avoiding and stopping the use of substances that will cause harm to our bodies. These substances include drugs and alcohol. A sober mind is quite a special and great tool in life. Alcohol is a stimulant, and sedative hence will influence the ability of the mind. It can also impair your perception and judgment at the moment. Other drugs are either stronger than alcohol, and hence their effect on the brain is higher, and therefore, the mental toughness is reduced or even doesn't exist in such individuals. If you are committed to making it in life and living a life that has no pressures, it is best you invest in yourself.

Those that are aware of their capacities will take good care of their bodies and will make sure the body is in a sane condition. While in a sober mind, it is easier to do exercises of the brain, read more, exercise better decision making, and be aware of yourself. A mind is a magical tool, and it will do magic if treated with the right treatment and conditions. Self-awareness and self-knowledge will be so helpful. Once you know who you are and what it is that you need in this world will help you gain the mental toughness to attain the goals set. Self-discipline will come in automatically to make sure the mental strength is well in place and installed.

Goals Commitment

A strong will to achieve the set goals and self-discipline will anchor you to your path, and no wavering will be observed. Without mental toughness, you will set your goals and outline your plans, but you will be swayed aware by other distractions. Commitment to the goals will need more than mental toughness, and here self-discipline kicks in. If your power of will and interests are in place, not forgetting the passion, all you now need is to lock mental toughness and work on your self-control. Commitments are important, and if they mean a lot to you, then you will sacrifice all that needs to be sacrificed. You will also make sure all team players towards your achievements are in unison as well as being in place. These team players are mental strength and self-discipline.

Focus is important. Mental toughness will require you to focus on the commitments put in order to attain the bigger picture, your goals. Mental toughness will make sure no laziness sets in, and you are all alert of the surroundings to ensure no opportunity goes untouched. With the mind alert, you now focus on other desires and distractions. Train yourself to say no so as to maintain the eyes on the prize ahead. Self-control will require you to take control of your emotions and physical desires and weigh them out to select only those that will add value to your goals. Be assertive and also selective. Emotional intelligence calls will also play a great role in maintaining feelings of anxiety or any other emotion that can be a distractor.

The medical field is a demanding area that requires full attention. Medical students have to be resilient and focus on the way to completion of their medical degrees or their equivalent. These students have self-discipline, and some have mental toughness. It is true to say that not all that get enrolled in medical school make it to the graduation time. The learning there is so much, a lot of memorization and activities that are monitored. Here, mental toughness and self-discipline will even make life easier. The combination will allow you to focus ahead and maintain cohesion with a colleague without much straining or pressure. A responsible and good doctor is one who has a sense of direction and has a feeling of self-dependency. Self-confidence is a trait that one acquires with more and more practice on mental toughness and self-control. Patients will feel safe in the hands of a doctor that will believe in himself, his skills, and experience rather than one that has to confirm of seeking permission to do a certain procedure. Boldness is key.

How to Increase Your Self-Discipline (Practical Advice)

Be aware of the weaknesses

Get to know of the weaknesses that you have, be it weaknesses in food, in clothing, in certain events, and get to know them so that you can devise proper ways in which you will deal with them. This is to ensure that they do not hinder you from accomplishing your set and planned goals. Your weaknesses could also be in things such as social media and the internet, and by getting to know them, you'll be in a better position to devise ways in which to avoid the distractions. You are not to give a cold shoulder on the fact that between you and your goals, there might be preferences that you hold dear to that could actually be stumbling blocks and hurdles to your achievement and being self-disciplined. In a nutshell, knowing your weaknesses will help you to be more self-disciplined.

Doing away with tempting factors

Once you identify the weak points that may hold you done from being self-disciplined, do away with them. It may not be easy to discard off things that you treasure dearly, but you must strive to do so, for they will just be holding you down from being fully set on self-discipline. Psyche up yourself to put behind the distractions, willing yourself to do so, and tapping into your inner owner when the temptation to hold on to them becomes too much.

Have well-set goals with a planner on how to implement them

Of importance to increase your self-discipline is to write down the plans and the goals that you have and have planner here you do so. Having goals and ambitions is a great motivator to become disciplined to reach the goals that you have set. Plan them, accordingly, making sure that you are comfortable with the time frame that you give yourself to achieve them. Planning them will be a more permanent way of a start on actualizing your goals, where self-discipline will be required. Last, but not least: Do not fear them.

Develop your self-discipline step by step

The skill of being self-disciplined is not one with which people are born with. It is one skill that will require your constant devotion in its build-up to increase its levels. Self-discipline is actually a behavior that you learn along the way in life, so, therefore, make a point to learn and incorporate self-discipline in your life. Self-discipline is well built up in situations where your will power and resilience are tested. Where the temptation to slump back I greater, that's where self-discipline is required in a great measure, and it would do you good to overcome the temptation, thus increasing your self-discipline.

Have new habits and practice on them

Greater levels of self-discipline would require you to form new habits and stick to doing them. Such habits of attaining higher standards are an uphill task to form at first, but with proper practice on them, they become a part of you that you do naturally. You become more at ease with them, and there is no strain on your part when doing them. Practice on them daily to be a part of your daily habits. You may want to go slow on yourself when practicing and not too hard, for they are new habits you are trying to instill in yourself.

Go healthy on foods and diet

Self-discipline requires a higher level of mental state, a clear and stable mind. Greater psychological power is required to be more self-disciplined. One of the factors that may increase your mental capacity is going healthy on your diet. The food you eat plays a huge and crucial role in strengthening or deteriorating your mental capacity. Healthy foods such as complex carbohydrates are great in maintaining your mind in great shape. Sugary foods, on the other hand, reduce your mental prowess, and should thus be avoided. With greater mental capabilities come a greater ability of self-discipline. Keep healthy and fit to be more self-disciplined.

Have a turnabout of your perception on resilience and willpower

Your thoughts on resilience and willpower are determinants to a great deal of how self-disciplined you will be. More willpower in situations will increase the self-discipline you have. Think about being more resilient in situations that require perseverance, and you will be more self-disciplined from the thoughts you feed your mind. Make yourself believe in them too.

Create a backup plan for situations

Draw up a plan that you will employ in situations that require your self-discipline. If you know that you are doing to delve into scenarios where your willpower will be tested, draw a plan in your mind to help you get through it. This is a technique to be prepared for the challenges testing your self-discipline. When you overcome such a situation, you will have boosted your self-discipline, which increases with every temptation that you face and overcome.

Acknowledge and appreciate yourself

When you have attained what you had planned for successfully, give yourself credit for the work well done. Having achieved a task, with no distractions whatsoever and not giving in to temptations, appreciate your efforts. This will keep you motivated and in good spirits, looking forward to the next task that you are to achieve. Anticipating for the next thing to do and the next objective to meet is a powerful tool in ensuring that you are on toes ready to focus. Praising yourself for the tasks accomplished with self-discipline motivates you to be more self-disciplined over future tasks.

Learn to forgive yourself over mistakes done and move on

When you have made a mistake, say where self-discipline was needed, but you did not employ it as required, learn to forgive yourself and let go of the self-loathing and bitter emotions. Fringing yourself gives you a chance to let go of past mistakes and taking them as lessons that you learn. From the lessons, you will learn how and when to apply self-discipline, thus increasing the self-discipline in you.

Chapter 6. Self-Discipline Starts from The Mind

Our mindset and individuality are tied together. Mindset is merely referring to your belief that qualities such as intelligence and talent are something that you can change or something that you are born with and cannot develop. The mindset becomes essential when you are looking at growth and change. If you feel that you are who you are and that cannot be changed, you have a fixed mindset. However, if you think that you can develop and strengthen opportunities that come your way, and you can develop abilities through being committed and working hard, your mindset is a growth mindset. People oftentimes have a mixture of both, and the way you think becomes the way that you are.

What Is the Mindset?

Looking at what your mindset is can determine different aspects of your life, your success, and your failures. If you have a positive mindset, you are more likely to succeed at the tasks you set out to accomplish. A negative mindset can be as debilitating as breaking a limb. You hold yourself back when you do not adopt a positive mindset.

Remember that you are able to change your mindset. You need to focus on the process rather than the outcomes and understand that effort, hard work, and dedication can lead to change. By doing this, you are giving yourself the gift of changing your mindset and thus changing your outcomes.

How Do Our Thoughts Affect Our Perception?

When you are trying to cope with the challenges that you face in life, your mindset is essential. You can experience more significant achievement with increased effort, and relying on a positive, growth mindset allows you greater resilience. You are less likely to give up when you face roadblocks or obstacles with a growth mindset. People with fixed mindsets often give up and need approval.

When looking at how your mindset affects how you see the world, it's essential to understand what perception is. Perception is simply giving yourself a prompt of what the world is like and how you can change it. As life is unfolding around you, it's your responsibility to determine if it is good or bad. This allows you a chance to lead or follow as you watch life unfold around you.

You can change your situation by changing the way you are looking at the situation that you are in. If you are experiencing something that is making you unhappy, consider trying to make it worse. Visualize yourself having something worse happened to you. How does this make you feel? Continue to visualize, making the situation work and feel the emotions that are associated with that. While this may be scary and is a powerful exercise that is going to allow you to look back at the situation you are in and reevaluate it. Figure out if the situation you are in is as bad as you see it.

Try to reframe how you see the world. Each time you encounter a situation that you feel is going to affect you negatively, continue to try to reframe your thoughts. Look at the situation from new angles and ask yourself questions about how you can change where you are. Remember that you control how a situation affects you, and you do not have to allow the negativity to permeate your world.

Start by changing your attitude. If you have a poor attitude, everything is going to seem worse than it is. Each setback is going to feel like it's in life and being, and you will not be able to move on. If you have a positive attitude, the situations that life throws at you will not be something that can stop you, but instead, they are going to be something that can spur you on and allow you to be successful.

You may not realize how powerful your mindset is. When you allow your changing to think, you are allowing your life to change. You can control your thinking, and you can make changes to how you view things and how you will enable them to affect you. The mindset that we have are necessary because we live the majority of our lives in our mind.

What Is Willpower?

The definition willpower is the ability that you have to control doing something or restraining your impulses.

Willpower plays a vital role in our lives. When you can resist the urge to do something, you are setting a habit in your mind of delaying gratification.

Often, people believe that they could have changed their outcomes if they only had more willpower. Understand that your lack of willpower may not be the sole reason that you are unable to meet your goals. Your motivation can also have something to do with that, and if you are afraid to fail, that can also affect how much you can accomplish.

Being able to resist temptations at the moment is going to allow you to meet your long-term goals. When you delay the gratification that you feel you need, you are setting yourself up to be successful. People who have weak willpower often

struggle with being consistent. They do not see the long-term effects of the choices that they make. They are often impulsive and fail to look past what is happening right now.

There are benefits to having strong willpower. If you exhibit strong self-control, you will have more excellent physical and mental health, fewer problems with substance abuse, and have better success financially. Understand that it does not matter where you are from; you can still find success if you learn to control your willpower.

How Can I Strengthen My Self-control?

An effective way to strengthen your self-control is by avoiding temptation entirely. If you know that you are not able to resist the urge, it is better to eliminate that possibility. Consider if you know that you binge eat on ice cream when you are sad, the best thing to do is not keep the ice cream in the house, correct? If you know you get distracted by having your phone handy while you are trying to work, the best solution is to keep the phone across the room from you. By avoiding the temptation, you are less likely to give in to the urge.

Another technique that you can use involves you using if-then statements. If I do this, then this will happen. An example would be if I save $50, then next weekend I will be able to go out. If I spend this $50, next weekend I will not have any money to enjoy. When you frame life with these types of statements, you are utilizing second-order thinking. By using second-order thinking, you can see the consequences beyond just what is going to happen now. Longer-term, this is a useful technique that allows you to delay the gratification that you seek.

What Is Individuality and How Does It Affect My Mindset?

Individuality is the qualities or characteristics that make a person or thing different from something of the same kind. Who you are is reflected in the traits and abilities that you possess? Not everyone is the same, and when you realize this, you will make choices that will affect you in a positive manner rather than making choices that are going to affect you negatively.

Individuality is what allows life to give us different experiences and allows for balance in the world. When you are trying to understand your individuality, this could cause you to become stuck because you are focusing on trying to meet expectations and standards that are outside of you. If you fail to see your limits, this will also hold you back. Understanding your individuality and how it is related to your current situation, is going to help you determine how to change where you are at.

Seeing yourself in reality, versus having delusional thinking about who you, is your mindset. Self-exploration is a great exercise that allows you to become more familiar with your

wants, your desires, your likes, and your dislikes. Doing this expands your sense of individuality and is going to be helpful to you when you are looking at your mindset.

Your mindset is going to determine our thinking patterns. Your thoughts control who you are, and they control how you see the world. If you do not know your place in the world, your mindset is going to be a negative one. Allow yourself the time and the energy that is needed to explore who you are authentically. Self-exploration is going to give you the gift of what is going to make you happy and what is holding you back at the moment.

How Do I Change My Mindset?

There are several techniques that you can use to give your mindset a boost. Determine first how your mindset is holding you back. This can manifest in several different ways, but the most common way is you feel that you are not making any progress towards who you want to be and how the world sees you. Along with exploring your individuality, it is crucial to figure out if you have a positive mindset or a negative mindset.

A positive mindset is going to allow you to make changes as needed, develop self-confidence that is unbreakable, and progress through life the way that you wish.

On the other hand, a negative mindset is going to hold you back. Fear, anxiety, and depression come along with a negative mindset. When you allow yourself to give in to the negative thinking patterns, you are holding yourself back from your dreams and your potential.

Self-talk

Self-talk is just the conversations that you have within yourself. These conversations directly reflect your mindset. If you are constantly criticizing yourself, it is impossible to have a positive outlook on life. These thoughts create and shape what your reality is, and they will hold you back from having the opportunities, the outcomes, and the experience that you desire. To change your self-talk, you need to stop the negative comments that you are allowing to form in your mind. Change these negative comments into an empowering speech that you give to yourself every time you start to doubt your ability. Tell yourself that you can do this, and I've got this.

You'll begin to see the change in your thinking, and this will result in changing the way you see the world. Your thought patterns will be shaped to embrace positivity.

The Language That You Use

After you can change your self-talk, you need to look at how you are talking to other people. Are you continually being negative when you speak with others? Do you find that you focus on the negative aspects of life rather than looking and embracing at the positive? Avoid complaining and avoid talking about the problems that you are experiencing. By doing this, you are encouraging a mindset that is going to embrace the abundant life that is out there. You will be able to stop your fear and your feeling of lacking and allow yourself to look on the bright side.

Learning Is Beneficial

Exploring material on mindset is beneficial. You can allow yourself to learn new techniques and new tips on how you can change and improve your mindset. Remember that your attitude and your mindset are very carefully related and that to have them function together, they needed to be in line with each other. You can have a positive attitude, but if your thinking patterns are negative, you are going to be off kilter. It sounds impossible to have a positive attitude and a negative mindset, but it is possible. As humans, we often fake an excellent attitude to avoid the repercussions of a negative one. Usually, our thoughts reflect our attitude, but sometimes that's not the case. Work hard to learn the different techniques and tips that are out there to improve your mindset and to change it, and you will begin to see positive changes in your life.

Combining a positive mindset and using the aspects of who you are as an individual is important. To be happy and successful in life, you need to combine both. Individuality defines who we are, how we are different from everyone around us, and why we are important. Losing your individuality is something that you must avoid at all costs. Embrace the quirks that make you unique and never apologize for being different!

Chapter 7. The Power of Habits In Self-Discipline

Self-discipline is a work-in-progress and a goal. The goal is to become more self-disciplined. However, being self-disciplined is not something one achieves once and considers it done. Once self-discipline is achieved, it must be considered a lifestyle—it must be nurtured daily and constantly refreshed to stay relevant and useful. Self-discipline is a habit—a good habit to have to make life more worthwhile.

Self-discipline is the backbone of a successful person. Whether a person desires personal success, professional success, or both, self-discipline will lead them to their goal. It begins with a strong ability to control oneself with strict discipline. Thoughts are under control. Emotions are under control. Behavior is under control. This does not mean that thoughts never run wild and emotions never flow to the surface. It just means that they are never allowed to control the person. One might get a little misty eyed at the birthday card with the cute kittens on it, but one would not let this feeling take over the entire day. This is self-discipline. The person controls thoughts and emotions. Self-control becomes a habit—a new personal best friend.

A burning desire to achieve these goals will not be enough to achieve these goals. Strong knowledge of personal strengths and weaknesses combined with a good understanding of how to discipline oneself is the key to being successful. Good habits make the difference between failure and success.

Successful people know that discipline is the key that unlocks the door to future goal achievement. They use discipline daily to enable themselves to be able to achieve their dreams. They know how to use a strong foundation built on strong habits to enable them to be successful. They are fully aware that self-discipline will allow them to accomplish more in less time—making them a more valuable member of the team.

But where does this discipline come from? How does one person seem so at-ease with controlling their actions and behaviors while other people fail on a daily basis? How do some people live lives of total self-control, while other people never seem to know where their shoes are, much less where they are going? The answer is habit. Behavior is mostly driven by habit. If someone can control their habits, they can have strict control over their personal habits.

Moreover, developing good habits really is as simple as knowing where the shoes are. A self-disciplined person would have a dedicated space for shoes. When the shoes are removed from the feet they are placed in this dedicated space. The self-disciplined person is never almost late to work because they cannot find their shoes. If this sounds familiar, then try this little exercise. Pick a dedicated place for the shoes. It does not matter where; the closet, tucked under the bed, next to the night stand, wherever. The dedicated spot is a personal choice. Now, every night, make a conscious effort to put the shoes in the dedicated spot every time they are removed from the feet. One day, it will be apparent that this has become a habit—a good habit to have—because now, there is no more searching for the shoes on cold, dark mornings. While this exercise may seem quite simple, it is a prime example of setting a goal, making a plan to achieve that goal, and achieving that goal.

Good habits will allow a person to create a good plan for achieving future goals. Without good habits, self-discipline will never become a reality. But how are these habits developed? Why is it so difficult to overcome bad habits?

The problem is the pathways in our brains. Whenever a habit is begun, whether it is a good habit or a bad habit, the brain creates pathways that tell the body to act a certain way when certain things happen. A cigarette smoker will want to light up a cigarette when someone else does. Seeing the cigarette, smelling the cigarette, triggers the nerve pathways in the brain of a smoker to have their own cigarette. This is why cigarette smokers who are trying to quit are often encouraged to change some of their daily habits. Smoking is often tied to other activities. Beer drinkers who smoke will smoke more when drinking. Coffee drinkers who smoke will automatically light up while pouring that first morning cup. People who smoke on long car trips may be encouraged to chew gum instead. People who drink may need to stop frequenting the local bar. Coffee drinkers will need to find something to do with their hands instead of lighting a cigarette. The nerve pathways that the bad habit created can be broken. It will take time and hard work. But then NOT smoking becomes the new good habit.

Creating good habits from bad requires effort but it can be done. Good habits take time to build and bad habits take time to break. Start small, work hard and consider a few simple tricks that might help ease into the habit of fostering good habits.

Start by taking the time to be thankful for what is already present in life. Humans spend much more time than needed wanting bigger, better things. Once people learn to be happy with the things they already have and not waste time wanting things they do not have, they can begin to see what is really important in life and begin to make a plan to add to those things that are really meaningful.

Humans spend far too much time feeling useless emotions like guilt or anger. Negative emotions use way too much energy that is needed to focus on the good things in life. Letting go of negative emotions frees the mind, the heart, and the soul to be able to focus on the positive effects that building new habits will create. Learning how to let go of negative emotions is actually an excellent way to build self-discipline. It is a way of letting the world see the strength inside.

Daily meditation has a wonderful effect on the ability to become more self-disciplined. Meditation leads to a clear mind, a relaxed heart. It improves physical and mental health. A few minutes of meditation daily leads the body to sync up better with the mind. It is much easier to create good habits that will lead to self-discipline if the mind is relaxed and ready to receive good thoughts.

It is important to set specific goals by writing them down. Once a goal is committed to paper it becomes an active thing, something that can be seen. Goals that are kept in the mind do not have the same strength as goals that are written down. Goals in the mind can be forgotten or pushed aside. Goals written on paper are seen every time the paper is seen—and when they are written down, it is impossible to ignore them. They want attention. They want direction and planning. They want to be considered, cared for and loved. They want attention. Start small and work on them daily.

Remember to eat healthily and sleep well and regularly. The body cannot process new habits if it is undernourished. Good healthy food is crucial to giving the body enough energy to work on new and better habits. This is especially necessary when trying to break bad habits. Bad habits require extra energy to put aside. Sleep is especially important too. Most adults need between seven and nine hours of sleep every night. Play around with these numbers until the correct amount is determined, and then stick to that number. Make every attempt to go to bed at the same time each night and wake up at the same time each day. This is a good habit that will lead to self-discipline of personal habits. Of course, things happen, and sometime people fall off the schedule. But get back on it as soon as possible and do not regret one or two small slips. They happen.

Exercise is another good habit that must be settled into the daily routine. Regular exercise is important in keeping the body healthy. Usually, the word 'exercise' gives bad connotations to many people. But exercise does not need to be a negative thing. It does not mean running out to join the neighborhood gym or begin training for a marathon. Anything that gets the body moving is exercise. Go for a walk, jump rope, play with the kids in the front yard—anything, just get moving. Join a sports team. Remember how much fun baseball used to be. Rake leaves, clean out the garage, push the lawn mower around the yard. Regular movement releases stress and tensions and is another way to create a good habit.

Practice organization. Some people are naturally organized, and some people need to work very hard to be organized. If the latter group seems more familiar, do not try to become completely organized overnight. The organization will not happen, but failure definitely will. Being well organized is a habit—and like any other good habit, it will take work to achieve. Begin by organizing one thing. Begin with a drawer. It is small and easy to organize. Have some boxes ready. When removing things from the drawer look at them closely and try to recall the last time they were used. If it has been more than six months, then the item is not needed. Have some boxes ready while doing this. If the item is still in good condition it goes in the box to be donated. If the item is beyond usefulness, then it goes into the box to go to the trash. Be firm! Do not hold onto something because it might get used. If it's a family heirloom and impossible to give up, put it in a box in the attic. When one drawer is clean, go to the next one. When all the drawers are organized move to the cabinets. As long as unnecessary items are not brought back into the house, then the house will remain clean and well-organized. Cleanliness will become a habit.

Time management is another goal that is necessary to embrace to build good habits and become self-disciplined. If there is no time management then time is the manager, and time is a very bad manager. Unmanaged time will slip away rapidly, leaving no time left in the day to do all the things that need to be done. Time management is nothing more than a plan to reach a goal of order and organization. An important part of time management is cleaning out the activities. Just like cleaning drawers of unused items, there are many unnecessary activities clogging up daily life. After the drawers and cabinets are cleaned and the house stays organized, one unneeded activity (constantly straightening the house) will be eliminated. It really is that simple.

Think of all the time that is actually wasted throughout the day engaging in unnecessary activities. How much time is wasted digging through a laundry basket looking for socks, when it would be so much quicker if the socks were in the drawer. How much time is wasted deciding what to cook for dinner when there is no set menu plan available to consult. How much time is wasted trying to find lost shoes? It all adds up.

No level of discipline will be successful without persistence. Temporary failure is not a reason to give up. Persistence is what keeps people going even through times of extreme failure. As far as progress goes, failure is an important part of life. Think of it not so much as doing something the wrong way but in finding yet another way that just did not work. In that instance, it is a learning opportunity and not a failure. This will also help lead toward greater self-discipline, by refusing to quit.

Habit and discipline go together hand-in-hand. Building a new habit is difficult in the very beginning because the body and the mind need to be taught a new way of thinking and working. But chasing good habits with persistence leads to greater self-discipline. The longer a habit is practiced, the more it becomes a part of the routine. It becomes easier. It becomes a habit, and no longer need to be practiced daily. It just naturally gets done—and once one new habit is set, it becomes much easier to add each successive one. If someone makes the decision to quit smoking, then not smoking is the new habit that will be cultivated. Once it has been persistently practiced long enough so that it is not so difficult anymore, then it is much easier to add healthy eating. After all, one good habit deserves another, right? With two new good habits in place, it just makes sense to add the habit of regular exercising. This is how new and better habits are formed and how habits build upon each other to create a lifestyle of self-discipline.

Self-discipline is nothing more than practicing a series of good habits until they become ingrained in the daily routine to the point where they are a part of life. As more bad habits are replaced with good habits, then the good ones take over and lead to a more orderly and organized life. As life becomes more organized, it becomes easier to manage—and now, it has become a life of self-discipline.

Chapter 8. Personal Successful Habits for Self-Discipline

Sexual Promiscuity

Everyone loves sex, but when it becomes the most important part of your life, abuse sets in. If you find yourself engaging in unhealthy sexual habits such as sleeping around with different sex partners, having sex without protection even when you know the dangers it exposes you and others to, engaging in sex for money no matter how hard the economic crunch has dealt with you, engaging in sexual acts in public places such as clubs, recreation parks, amusement parks, alleys, lobbies, shopping malls, parking lots, school premises, classrooms, offices, toilets, etc. If you find yourself unable to keep your sexual urge under control to the point that you throw all decency and decorum to the winds, know you need to do something to increase your level of self-discipline.

Drunkenness

If you find yourself in love with alcohol to the point that you place it above everything else, it is a good sign you are not disciplined. No one is saying you should not drink alcohol; the point is in applying moderation in everything you do. Know the level of alcohol your system reacts to and the level of alcohol that can make your system lose control of its normal functions and behaviors and do not go over that limit. If you find yourself longing for alcohol more than you long to become a better or a more successful you, then you must take urgent steps to address the issue before it gets out of hand.

Laziness

This one is among the significant indiscipline signs you can find in any individual. If you are self-disciplined, you will find it difficult to hold on to your bed when others are out there looking for how to make ends meet. A disciplined man knows when to jump out of bed, get dressed, fold his sleeves, and get to work. If you find yourself lazing about when you should either be studying or working, then you need to help yourself before the world leaves you behind.

Procrastination

This one goes hand-in-hand with laziness. If you are lazy, the next thing for you to do is to put everything away until a later and a more convenient time. If you find yourself procrastinating and leaving everything until a later time, you lack self-discipline. People with self-discipline understand the importance of starting every task on time and staying put until they have accomplished it. Procrastination is one of the reasons why indiscipline remained a vice that has robbed many of their once bright destinies. Whenever you find yourself leaving until tomorrow what you can conveniently begin or accomplish today, it shows you lack self-discipline.

Cheating

If you cheat, you lack self-discipline, and there will always be a limit to what you can achieve in life. No one has ever recorded success on anything in life while cutting corners. Cutting corners might get you there fast, but in reality, it will always get you off the top more quickly than it got you there.

Impatience

If you are fond of trying to rush things when they require a little patience for perfection to be achieved, you lack self-discipline and you can hardly get anything done with perfection.

Lack of diligence

Have you seen a man diligent in his work? That man has self-discipline. It is common to experience challenges in your line of work or business. Even if you are still studying, there comes a time when you experience unusual setbacks that require you to be diligent and persevere. If you are self-disciplined, you will see obstacles as opportunities to work harder to come out with a better result than you were working towards.

Selfishness

Selfish people are not self-disciplined. If you are always thinking about your own good, even when it is to the detriment of everyone else, it shows you need to sharpen your self-discipline more. Selfishness is one thing that can give you instant gratification but hurt you in the long run. It is a self-discipline that helps you share what you have with others.

Gluttony

Greed is also a common bad habit that shows you lack self-discipline. Gluttony and greed are the same concepts focused on different objectives. Gluttony is often referred to as food and greed to possessions and success. A greedy person is never going to be self-disciplined due to the consequences it has, and this can be illustrated in several ways.

Have an Attitude of Gratitude

Gratitude comes with a whole lot of benefits, from improving the state of your mental health to enhancing your emotional wellbeing. Most importantly, gratitude helps you detach from your state of lack and scarcity. Thinking about the things you desire which you have not been able to get will make it hard for you to attain the level of self-discipline you need to achieve your goals.

Forgive

When it comes to forgiveness, you must learn to forgive both yourself and others to enable you to get ahead in life. Learning to forgive yourself when you err and others when they hurt you, help build up your energy for success and makes you more disciplined. Whenever people hurt you, forgive them and empty your mind of a load of hate and malice. Forgiving people who hurt you helps you release all negative energy that makes you lose your self-discipline. Please, you must get rid of the negative energy, because holding it will make you feel tired, discouraged, and angry all the time, plus it subtracts you the capability of thinking.

Meditation

Engaging in meditation helps put your mind at ease. It creates a type of spiritual atmosphere around you to help you grow and become a better you. Meditation sets the stage for you to attain a higher state of self-discipline by clearing the palette of your mind and putting you in the right mood to face the challenges of the day.

Set Active Goals for Each Day

Active goals are active because they can be seen. You make your goals active by putting them down on paper and placing them where they can be seen. Active goals help you build and increase your level of self-discipline because they give your daily life directions. This is when I talk about daily activities. There's no need to have an extreme objective or dream to set active goals; in fact, there are activities, such as washing the clothes, reading books, cooking, sleeping 8 hours a day, etc. that you will need to do every day. You can start with those home activities to increase your self-discipline.

Eat Right

When you eat the right foods, you help your body store more energy. When your diet is mostly composed of fats, carbohydrates, and proteins, your body dissipates lots of energy processing such foods. Also, having the schedule of meals and with this, I mean eating on time, will help you to have a healthy life when it comes to ingesting the right aliments at the right time. This way, you will avoid having diseases or stomach problems, such as gastritis. Having these health problems will only take part of your time to recover, and you will have to postpone the activities of your goals.

Get Enough Sleep

Whether you give your body enough rest by getting adequate sleep or not goes a long way to determine your ability to stay focused on your goal to achieve self-discipline and your general wellbeing.

Exercise Daily

Incorporating physical exercises into your daily routines helps you get rid of bad habits and adopt positive practices. If you want to learn to discipline yourself, make specific physical exercises part of your morning routine. Most people give the excuse that they are too busy or have a lot of worries to get involved in physical activities. Where such people get it wrong is that they forget they can improve their entire lives through physical exercises.

Stay organized

Don't just wake up and start working on your goals for the day. Make sure you have your goals and daily tasks arranged in an orderly manner. Arranging your goals in an orderly manner helps you stay organized, which is a good sign of self-discipline. Being organized goes beyond having a list of things to do, taking into account priorities. It also involves organizing all areas of your life such as your work table, your drawer, your kitchen cabinets, your wardrobe, your garage, your bedroom, and all other such spaces in your life.

Read

The body is not everything, and health does not imply only to work out the collection. You also have to work out your mind and improve your knowledge and intelligence. There's nothing better to do this than reading a book. It is considered one of the best habits a person may have and will definitely; definitely guide you to get your goals. It is always recommended to read a book often. You will learn from it, and you will find different ways to perform your daily activities. Besides, you can find encouragement in this, improve your reading and writing skills, your orthography and you'll feel more confident in any aspect of your life, due to the acquired knowledge.

Chapter 9. Traits Of A Navy SEAL

In many ways, your journey toward improved self-discipline is a journey toward becoming a whole new person. That doesn't mean that you have to leave everything about your current self in the past – there is certainly a lot of great things about the person you are today. However, if you wish to add in a strong dose of self-control in order to strive toward your ultimate goals, making changes is going to be a necessary step.

Every person who successfully becomes a Navy SEAL comes out of the experience a completely changed person as compared to when they started. Specifically, they have acquired a list of twelve traits that will carry them through everything they do as a SEAL and beyond. These ten traits are listed below – as you work toward a new sense of self-discipline, monitor your progress against the presence of each of these traits. When you feel like you represent each of these twelve points in your day to day life, you will know that you have made great strides toward living like a SEAL.

Confident

Confidence is essential to success in any walk of life. You can be sure that SEALs have confidence when they undertake a mission, and you should be looking to find the confidence within yourself. Everyone has confidence inside of them, and it will only come out when the right daily habits are in place. When SEALs are confident, they instill confidence in their team members. It's important for them to be 100% sure of themselves and to never be cocky. Overconfidence can come off as arrogance and when this happens the entire team can be set up for failure.

Decisive

If you don't act quickly, someone else will. SEALs are problem solvers who thrive in a setting called VUCA. This stands for Volatility, Uncertainty, Complexity and Ambiguity and is also referred to as the "fog of war." Sometimes you just need to trust your gut and rely on your preparation to make the call. Wrong decisions are going to be made. This is a fact of life. SEALs come prepared and make quick, calm and calculated choices. They will correct an error and move on to the objective. Hesitation and indecision can get a SEAL or his team killed. Decision making is another trait which can define you as a self-disciplined person. There is no time for hesitancy in the life of a person with big goals to meet.

Assertive

Being assertive has a lot to do with being confident. You don't have to be rude to be assertive - you just have to be sure enough in yourself to stand up for what is right. The best SEALs are aggressive but not overbearing. Ask for what you need and the universe will respond.

Strong

SEALs are selected on 4 must have strength traits. These are moral courage, problem solving, team ability and of course physical strength.

Strength in life is important – SEALs maintain an extreme level of physical and mental strength to consistently find success.

Skillful

Developing elite performers means ruthless competition, and most aspirants do not make the grade. The word Skillful is almost an understatement when you have become a US Navy

SEAL. The skills needed by the SEALs are specific to the military actions that they are going to undertake. For you, it may be skills in business or sales that are required to move through your career with success. There are certain skills that you need to acquire in order to reach your goals, and those skills will be specific to whatever it is in life that you want to accomplish. Whatever those skills are, you must pursue them aggressively until they are able to support your mission.

Calm

During the second phase of BUD/S, students are required to perform underwater activities and execute a variety of emergency procedures while wearing scuba gear. During the exercise, the instructors attack the students and disconnect the gear, leaving them deep underwater without any equipment. The students that remain calm and do not panic are the only ones to pass the test. They are able to function longer underwater by staying calm. To prepare for this, they perform concentrated breathing exercises and actually visualize the attack happening to them before entering the water. Mental visualization is important because when done repeatedly, it teaches and rewires your brain at a very primal level.

Disciplined

There might not be a more disciplined group of people anywhere on the planet than the Navy SEALs. Above all else, they are dedicated to their process and dedicated to their brothers with whom they serve. If you are going to get anywhere in life, it is going to be discipline that is going to take you there. For SEALs, discipline starts every morning at 5am when the alarm clock goes off. This is like a daily measurement tool that points out how you're operating. If you push snooze a few times you are demonstrating weakness, and this will show up in multiple areas during the day and in your life. If you get up on the first alarm you are more likely to have that momentum push during the day as well as having a little more time to work with. A small act of daily discipline can ripple outward and affect many areas of your life.

Adaptable

You probably think about SEALs as being regimented and carefully planned - which they are - but they are highly adaptable as well. It is important to understand that situations will change which will require you to change on the fly, even if that means adjusting your carefully laid plans. SEALs are taught to forget about motivation and rely on discipline. When put into a chaotic overwhelming situation they will simply prioritize tasks and execute. A dozen problems cannot be dealt with all at once so they will need to be handled one at a time. Choose the highest priority and handle it. When the battlefield changes, the course of action must change. Prioritize and execute.

Vigilant

A big part of the reason that SEALs are so successful out in the field is that they are never caught off guard. Vigilance as a trait means that you always have your 'eyes on the prize', and you are always ready to jump into action when needed. If you want to take advantage of opportunities as they emerge, even if they are unexpected, you will need to be vigilant on a day to day basis. SEALs make the unknown familiar. They do this by exposing their bodies to extremely cold temperatures and by using mental visualization to conceptualize themselves in a nasty firefight

Patient

There is nothing more important to a Navy Seal than understanding the virtue of patience. Self-Discipline like a

SEAL requires immense patience. A SEAL sniper can wait on a target for days if necessary. Calm yourself down and wait out the traffic jam you are in. No one can trust someone who indulges in their emotions. Staying calm will give you the ability to read and understand the situation before you make your move. This is a very good way of preventing wrong decisions that we often regret later. SEALs are patient with frustration from being fatigued and they are patient during duress.

Prepared

The devil is in the details. The first step to tactical problem solving is being detail-oriented and creating a robust plan. SEALs will spend countless hours preparing for combat. They will analyze the mission and get clear on what the specific objective is. Then they will identify personnel, assets, resources and time. Create a plan of action. Prepare for likely contingencies through each phase of operation. They will then delegate portions of the plans to key junior leaders. Then finally, they will brief the plan. This involves asking questions and engaging in discussion. Life and the battlefield will never goes as planned. Long term success is a thinking man's game. Being prepared is essential if you are going to reach your goals, so remember to rely on your level of discipline and not your level of motivation.

The navy seals who killed Osama Bin Laden were the same team that rescued the American Ship Captain Richard Phillips who was held hostage by Somalian pirates in 2009. SEAL snipers fired 3 precision shots in the dark from the rocking stern of the Norfolk destroyer Bainbridge, Killing all 3 targets instantly.

Chapter 10. Build Willpower

When you have strong willpower, you control your impulses. You know what you need to do to reach your goal or get the job done. Willpower is an important part of self-discipline because it helps you focus on what you need to do instead of what you want to do.

Everyone has some type of willpower. You might have the willpower to help you get tasks done when you are close to your deadline. You might find that your willpower is stronger when you first receive your task and get it started than when you are approaching the deadline. While some people can tell themselves "no" easily and follow through with their decision, other people don't have that strong of willpower and find themselves bending to their desires.

Two Main Parts of Building Willpower

There are two main parts when it comes to building willpower. The first part is motivation, and the second part is tracking your progress. Through these two factors, your willpower will slowly build and help you stay on track with your goals.

Before we discuss the two main parts, it is important to take time to discuss consistency. While this has been briefly mentioned before, when you are working on willpower, you need to make sure that you follow through with your plan every time. For example, for every goal you set, you want to have some type of tracking system that shows the progress you have made. By remaining consistent in these efforts, your goal setting and tracking system will become more of a habit than something you need to do. You will want to follow through with the system because you understand the benefits and you know what the outcome will be if you continue to remain consistent.

An example of how important consistency is and what it can do for you is the story of Samantha. As a freshman in college, Samantha struggled to make her classes. She felt that because everyone posted the work online and attendance was not part of her grade, she didn't need to go to class all the time. Instead, she would go to class if she needed to hand in an assignment, talk to her professor because she was having a problem understanding her classwork, or when there was a test or quiz. Samantha also told herself that if she found her grades were lower than a B, she would go to the class until her grades improved and then she could start to miss classes again.

Because Samantha found herself missing so many class periods, she didn't meet a lot of new people. When she did show up to class, she felt out of place and that everyone knew she hadn't been in class lately. She felt that the professor judged her for only coming to class on certain days. She started to believe that no one thought she would graduate from college.

Because Samantha missed so many classes, it quickly became a habit. She soon found herself missing important days, such as a day a quiz was scheduled because she didn't remember when her classes were. Soon, Samantha's habit was to miss classes instead of going to classes. At the end of the semester, Samantha received word that she was on academic probation and would be kicked out of school if she didn't improve her grade point average to 2.5.

After talking to her older sister, Samantha realized that her willpower to go to class diminished because she rarely went. Therefore, she felt it took more energy to go to class than to stay home and complete the assignments online or give her professor an excuse that she wasn't feeling well so she could make up a quiz. Samantha's sister told her that she needs to consistently go to class to build her motivation for her classes. Once she became more motivated, she would find that she wanted to make it to her classes.

The next semester Samantha made it a goal that she would only miss classes for an emergency or when she was sick. She wrote down in her planner whenever she made the class and when she struggled to find the energy to go to class, Samantha looked back at her planner to see that she hadn't missed class yet. Feeling proud of herself, she continued to go to class. By the fourth week of class, Samantha felt she had to get to class. When she came down with the flu in the sixth week, she felt bad for missing class and struggled to stay home and take care of herself instead of going to class.

For Samantha, remaining consistent in going to class and tracking the days she went to class, kept her motivated to continue the process. At the end of the semester, Samantha found herself on the Dean's List and rarely missed a class during the remainder of her college career.

Motivating Yourself

It is true, it is easy to motivate other people. It is hard to motivate yourself because it is easier to tell yourself, "I can do this later, I will have time," or "I can think about this tomorrow when I feel better and more motivated. Everyone deserves a day off." It is easier to listen to someone when they tell you to remain motivated or go to class because you don't want to disappoint them. You want your parents, friends, siblings, or significant others to be proud of you. Therefore, you tend to listen to their requests over your own.

Motivating yourself is an important part of your daily life. You need to motivate yourself to get up when your alarm goes off. You need to motivate yourself to make supper after a busy day. You need to motivate yourself to work instead of surfing the internet. You probably don't even realize all the times you need to motivate yourself throughout the day.

There are several techniques you can use to help motivate yourself:

Get Positive. It is easier for other people to motivate you because they are excited and positive. Some people feel silly when they try to make themselves feel excited and positive about a task they need to take on. However, it is essential to help get yourself motivated. The more excited and positive you are about completing the task, the more motivation you will have to focus on the task. Give yourself a pep talk if you need to. You can stand in front of the mirror to do this or talk to yourself out loud.

Surround yourself with people that will pressure you. Talk to people, such as your friends and family, about your goals. Ask them if they will be your sense of support when you are working on the task. If they want to see you succeed, they will agree to be your support. Tell them that there will be times they need to pressure you to get the job done or make sure that you are on track with your progress.

Always give yourself rewards. Once you complete a step or a task, give yourself a reward. The reward is there to keep you motivated so you continue working on the next part of your task or move on to a new goal.

Get started, as the motivation will come. You might be one of those people who finds motivation once they get a project started. If you like to see a project through to the end, it might be helpful to start the project and then look for your motivation. Chances are, you will find it as now that you have started the project, you need to make sure you finish it.

Get motivated through music. If you are the type of person that likes to work with background noise, you might find yourself more motivated to work when you have some of your favorite songs playing in the background. It is important to analyze if music will really help you with motivation and what type of music. For example, Amirah can concentrate on a task while listening to some of her favorite songs while Roger finds himself becoming distracted as he would rather listen to music than work. Therefore, Roger listens to classical or relaxing music that plays softly in the background.

Compare yourself to yourself. Like most people, you are probably good at comparing yourself to other people. You see your co-workers working hard at their tasks and wonder why you don't have this motivation yourself. You compare yourself to your friends who have more money, a bigger home, and nicer cars. You wonder why you can't get to that point and if it is because you don't work as hard. Instead of comparing yourself to other people, it is time to compare yourself to you. Look at your progress and think about the person you used to be when you first started the job. For example, Roger didn't have the confidence as a writer when he first started that he does now. Because of this confidence, Roger has become a stronger writer. When Roger compares himself, he notices how far he has come and can't help but become more motivated to continue his path.

Recording Your Progress

There are different ways to track your progress and it is important to focus on a method that works for you. The key is to be consistent with your method as this will keep you motivated to record your progress on a task every day. You want to do something that is comfortable and will work with your lifestyle. For example, Roger doesn't have to worry about getting ready for bed or putting kids to bed, so he records his progress after his evening meal. Amirah has a hectic schedule that often takes her away at certain times of the day. She doesn't always know when she will be home and when she won't, so she records her progress right before she goes to bed.

• **Start at zero but set a daily goal.** This method helps when you are trying to increase your exercise, or you want to walk many miles a day. The key is to always start at zero and try to reach a daily goal. For example, if you have a Fitbit, you have a certain number of steps you want to reach every day. At midnight, your watch starts at zero and records every step you make throughout the day. When you reach your goal, your watch makes a noise or vibrates, letting you know that your goal is met. This is the same idea you want to follow with other goals. For instance, you want to exercise for 30 more minutes every day. You will start at zero and then see how many minutes you exercised by the end of each day. You will record this progress in a journal or through a data tracker.

• **Journaling.** One of the most common methods of tracking progress is to write in a journal. You don't have to spend a lot of time writing in the journal every day, most people can detail their progress within five minutes. However, it is important that you take the time to write about your progress, even if you are more tired than usual or don't feel like writing that evening. You don't want to put it off until morning because you could forget to write down important tracking information and you get out of your system. You don't want to write about different goals on the same page as this can become confusing when you look back at your progress.

- **Excel spreadsheet or Microsoft Word**. Another way you can track your progress is by creating an excel spreadsheet or using Microsoft word. Doing this allows you to create a document that works for your system and keep it updated when you are on your computer. For example, you might find the best time to track your work progress is at the end of your workday.

There are four main steps when it comes to tracking your progress, no matter what method you use:

Look at the bigger picture. When you go through your day, you often follow the same pattern. This can lead to mindless thoughts and keep you from focusing on what you need to do. When you look at the big picture as you track your goals, you ask yourself a series of questions, such as "What do I want to accomplish?" and "What do I need to do to get my day started?" By thinking about these questions, you will visualize the result you want. This will get you started on focusing on your tasks and help you know what factors you need to consider when you are tracking your progress.

Organize and plan your time. Get a planner to help you stay on track with your goals. Write down what you want to achieve every day when it comes to your goals. Even if you only want to achieve calling your friends to see if they will become a source of motivation, you want to write this down. After all, part of reaching your goals is having a support network. When you know how long it should take you to reach your milestones, write them in your planner. For example, if you want to get to the second milestone in 10 days, write this down.

Don't do this alone. You need to find a partner that wants to focus on the same goal or someone that will be your accountability partner. This person can help you stay on track by motivating you to continue and helping you understand your progress. They can look to see where you are with your progress and notice if you are on track or not.

Remember to celebrate your success. You want to write down your celebrations just as you do your progress.

You Will Feel Drained

You don't want to read that a task you are taking on will make you feel drained. However, it is important that you understand working toward self-development, even when you are focusing on small steps can make you feel overwhelmed. You will have moments where you want to throw in the towel because you don't think you can accomplish your goal. You will have moments when your self-confidence seems low because you start bringing yourself down with your thoughts about how you aren't on track with your goal and you are a failure.

Emotions and mental work drain us and working toward a goal is mental and emotional work. You don't have to have a labor-intensive job to feel tired at the end of a workday. People who have a mentally intensive job can feel just as drained as people with a physically intensive job. It is not a competition and you should never feel that you don't work as hard as someone who works construction.

Another way working toward self-discipline is draining is because you are trying to better yourself. This requires a lot of focus and more work than you are used to. Even though recording your progress might only take five to ten minutes out of your day, you can feel drained when you need to reflect on your day every evening.

It is important that you realize the effort and focus you put toward your self-discipline and all its step is draining, but this should not scare you away. In fact, if it does, this should give you more motivation to focus on developing your self-discipline.

No matter how drained you feel at the end of the day, you have made progress and have increased your self-discipline. This is one reason why tracking your progress is so important, it helps you stay focused, especially during the tough days where you feel like you aren't making any type of progress.

If you go through a day where you don't focus on any of your progress, it is important that you don't take this to heart. Everyone has days when trying to find motivation is harder than any other task that day. Instead of emotionally and mentally beating yourself up over it, you want to think about it as a mental health day of progress. You needed a break, which everyone does from time to time. Take your mental health day and focus on reenergizing yourself for the next phase in mastering your self-discipline.

You Must Be Willing to Fail

Failing is not easy, especially when you are focused on a task and want to do your best. However, you need to remember that you can't have success without failures. When you fail, this gives you an opportunity to learn and grow. The key when it comes to failures is to fall forward. This means that you will use the opportunity to improve your weaknesses and learn from your mistakes. Even some of the most well-known movie stars received rejections, especially in their early days. Some of them have movies that didn't make it to the big screen while others are open about the failures they have had in their careers. Remember, when you fail, you are not alone in this process as everyone fails at some point within their lives — many times throughout their lives at that.

Chapter 11. Proven Methods for Gaining Self Discipline

Identify Clear Goals

By setting smaller goals, it becomes something that is more quantifiable, and because of this, you can easily keep track of how you are doing when it comes to goal achievement.

Active goal setting is very different from passive goal setting. Passive goal setting means you are setting goals in your mind, and they are passive because they lack many details are planning. Passive goal setting means that a person hasn't properly defined the actual goal, which makes it hard for them to keep track of their progress and knowing what needs to be done in order to achieve that goal. Active goal setting is the complete opposite of passive goal setting. Active goal setting means writing out these goals and making sure that they have an important meeting. These goals have to be measurable and very specific. To successfully have an active goal, a person has to make a plan towards achieving it. This is why people set long-term goals, but also engage in smaller goals on a daily basis in order to work towards achieving the bigger goal.

By using active goal setting, it ingrains the discipline in us because you are forced to give it direction. By breaking down your big goals into smaller daily goals, it helps people avoid distractions by only looking at the things that they need to get done in the present day. This way, a person isn't left constantly thinking about one large intimidating goal but not knowing how to approach it.

Active goal setting works by taking the first step in setting your long-term goals. If you are someone that has long-term goals like; wanting to own your first home, wanting to pay off your student debt by the next three years, or wanting to take 6 months off to travel Europe. If you are someone that has long-term goals, then you need to actively participate in daily, weekly, and monthly goal setting and planning. You have to play an active role in tracking your progress towards your goals and making changes in places wherein you feel like things aren't working for you.

So, take out a pen and a piece of paper and start writing down what long-term goals you have. Once you have some long-term goals written down, break it down into monthly, weekly, and daily goals. Start slowly by accomplishing your daily goals, and when you reach the end of the month, assess to see if you have achieved your monthly goal through accomplishing your daily goals. If you haven't, look back on your daily goals and see if there's anything you can change so that you could achieve next month's goal.

You have a list of tasks you want to accomplish. However, it seems that your list of goals continues to grow without you marking any of them off. You start to wonder if you will ever reach some of the goals you set for yourself. As you think about some of your goals, you realize how big they are, but you know you can achieve them—you are not always sure how, but you know it is possible.

One of the biggest practices when maintaining self-discipline is to create smaller steps for your goals. It doesn't matter how small you think your goal is, you always want to break it down into smaller steps. Think of your goal as the top of your stairs and each step you take is reaching one of the smaller goals that will lead you to achieve your main goal.

You don't want to make the mistake of setting your goal and finding yourself struggling to reach it because you didn't understand how to get started, what to do, or that the goal is too big for you. When you find yourself struggling with your goals, you are more likely to believe that you can't reach them. This will affect you psychologically and damage some of the self-discipline you have built.

Golden Goal Setting Rules

To help you get into the mindset of developing smaller goals within a larger goal, it is important to understand the golden rules when it comes to setting goals.

Write Down Your Goals

How often have you written down your goals, compared to keeping them locked away in your mind? You probably discuss your goals with family, friends, co-workers and other people in your life, but have you ever sat down and written out your goals? If not, physically writing out your goals can help make your goal real to you. While you might feel you want to achieve your goal when you think about it, you have thousands of thoughts going through your mind a day. You might have an idea of how to reach your goal, but how much work you put toward your goal every day? Have you ever forgotten about any goals you want to accomplish or pushed them to the side because you didn't feel they were important enough or you were too busy to focus on them? If so, the real reason you might have forgotten or pushed them away is because you didn't write them down.

When you write your goals down on paper, you want to use words like "will" instead of "might." You want to make the goal as concrete as possible. For example, instead of writing, "I would like to exercise for 30 minutes each day" you write, "I will exercise for 30 minutes every morning."

When you write down your goals, you want to frame them positively. You will write the way you think about your goal, so if you aren't completely sure you will reach your goal this will come out in your writing. Then, when you look at your written goals, you won't feel as strongly about achieving them, especially if you place doubt in your goals. For example, you write, "I will try to stick to my diet and say goodbye to all the yummy food," it isn't a motivational goal. You can feel negatively about this goal because it will make you feel that you are saying goodbye to your favorite foods and forcing yourself on this diet. You want to word the goal in a way that highlights your new diet positively. For example, you write, "I will stick to my diet to improve my overall health."

Use the SMART Rule

You can create goals or SMART goals. SMART stands for the five characteristics that every goal should be expressed as:

● **Specific**. Specific goals are well-defined and clear. You know exactly what you want and what steps you will take to reach your goal.

● **Measurable.** You want to include a plan to measure the progress of your goal. For example, you will have dates that give you a timeline of your goal. If you want to exercise for 30 minutes every morning, you will start by exercising 10 minutes every morning for two weeks. You will then increase your time by 5 minutes once a week until you reach 30 minutes.

● **Attainable.** Always know that you can achieve the goals you set. Of course, they can seem overwhelming at first, but your confidence will make you believe you can reach your goals. At the same time, you have to ensure that you need to work hard to achieve your goals. If you set goals that are too easy, you won't feel accomplished or grow out of your comfort zone.

● **Relevant.** Make sure your goals are relevant to the direction you want to take in your life. This will help you stay focused on your life's path and reach where you see yourself in three or five years.

- **Time-Bound.** Always make sure your goals have a deadline. The deadline might be in a month or three years. It all depends on the goal and its steps.

Your Goals Need to Keep You Motivated

If you set goals that don't motivate you to work on them, your goal setting won't work. You need to ensure that your goals are important to you and direct you where you want to go in life. If you don't imagine the outcome of your goals or have little interest in them, you need to look at why. Are you thinking about your goal in the right way? Are your goals something that you want to gain in your life? Is your goal a priority?

You need to have the "I must accomplish this goal" attitude to maximize the likelihood of achieving your goals. The result of not following this rule will leave you frustrated and disappointed in yourself.

Creating an Action Plan

Creating an action plan for each goal will help you follow through with them. You will remain excited and each step you accomplish will give you more motivation to achieve your goal. It's not easy to look at a goal and then think about your action plan. To help you get more comfortable with this process, here are some tips to incorporate as you create your plan.

Make sure your goals are clear and you know exactly what you want. Think about how you will describe your goal. Ensure that your goal is relevant to your life plans and attainable.

Create the steps to reach your goal by going backward. For example, if you want to eliminate your debt within a year, you will look at how much you need to pay off every month, every three months, and during the sixth month period. Having an amount for each of these milestones will help you keep better track of the steps of your goal. Make sure you include a timeframe for each step.

Take each step one by one and focus on it. You need to determine what actions are required for you to reach your goal. For example, you will create a budget and notice where you can save money or what money you can put toward your debt every month.

Ask yourself what reward you want to give yourself once you achieve each step and reach your goal. This reward needs to be something that will keep you motivated and something you don't give yourself regularly.

Create a daily plan. Ask yourself what you can do every day to make sure you reach your milestones and goals? For example, if you purchase a lunch at work every day, how much money will you save if you pack a lunch from home? Will meal planning help you stick to the schedule? What other daily habits do you have that can help you save money or put it toward your debt?

It is common to feel like you have a chaotic paper full of goals and scribbles when you are done creating your plan. If you need to re-write your plan it is best that you do. You want your plan to look clear and easy to follow as this will keep you motivated.

Make sure that you remain consistent in your daily schedule. This will help you achieve your milestones. Follow through with the tasks that you give yourself and remember to stay away from your rewards until you complete a step.

The biggest key when it comes to reaching your goals is to focus on one milestone at the time. Even when you look at your whole goal on the sheet, you want to keep your mind focused on the milestone you are working on at that moment. This will help keep you focused, and you won't feel so overwhelmed by your goal.

When Roger wrote his action plan to help him follow a schedule, he decided to observe his natural behavior for a week and note anything that helped him follow through with his schedule and anything that kept him away from his schedule. The helpful behavior and actions that Roger wrote down included:

- Getting up by 7:00 A.M. and getting dressed.

- Having a healthy breakfast.

- Sitting at my desk by 8:00 A.M.

- Switching my phone on silent and keeping it in another room.

- Keeping the television in my office area/bedroom off.

- Taking a 10-minute break to walk around the apartment every hour, but not turning on the television or sitting down.

- Taking a one-hour lunch break where I leave my work and focus on a relaxing activity.

- Stop working at 6:00 P.M. and relaxing or focusing on other activities the rest of the night instead of continuing to work late or going back to work after an hour.

The behaviors and actions Roger noticed that didn't help him stick to his schedule included:

- Staying up late and allowing myself to sleep in.

- Staying up too late and napping during the day.

- Eating a heavy and unhealthy breakfast.

- Not getting ready for the day, such as starting work while still wearing pajamas.

- Keeping my phone next to me.

- Keeping the silent mode off.

- Having non-work tabs open online.

- Turning on the television or watching a YouTube video when I am on a break.

- Not leaving my desk during my break.

- Working from the time I get up until I go to bed. This decreases my willpower to work the next day.

- Snacking often.

- Taking more than my needed breaks.

- Not standing up to the point when I feel the need to move.

- Telling myself that "I can work on it later in the day. I have time."

Once Roger had a clear understanding of what behaviors and actions helped him and which ones didn't, he started to create his plan. His goal became "I will follow my work schedule of starting at 8:00 A.M. and working until 6:00 P.M. with one 10-minute break every hour and a one-hour lunch break."

Roger then started to write out the steps of his goal. He gave himself a month to accomplish the goal and felt this was an adequate amount of time. The steps Roger included to help him make his goal were:

Start going to bed at 11:00 P.M and set an alarm to get up at 7:00 A.M

Get up and get ready for the day, just as I would when working outside of my home.

Have a healthy breakfast, such as fruit and eggs with a slice of bacon or a sausage patty.

Sit at my desk at 8:00 A.M.

Work until 8:55, when I will take a break until 9:05. Repeat this break every hour.

Take lunch at 11:55 A.M and be back to work at 12:55 P.M.

Stop working at 6:00 P.M.

Roger focused on giving himself a few days and worked on one step at a time. Once he went to the next step, he rewarded himself with his favorite ice cream treat. When he reached his goal of keeping to his daily schedule for a week ahead of his deadline, he allowed himself to take a vacation day. Roger continues to follow this schedule and he has found working from home to be more enjoyable as he separates his workday from his personal time with the schedule.

Create New Habits By Breaking Bad Habits

Getting rid of bad habits is the fastest way to begin creating the personality you need to tackle any task and get things done.

Habits are not always easy to quit. It becomes second-nature and might take having people that can help hold you accountable. Use post-it notes and calendar reminders to break tougher habits of putting off projects or poor time management.

Starting good habits

Beginning new habits that are good and productive might be as difficult as stopping the bad ones. The difference will be in your experience of positive benefits from good habits. Leaving to appointments on time, never being late to the job, always getting started on projects right away are all habits that will provide nearly immediate positive results. Sticking with your new routine and habits for 21 to 30 days will ensure that they are there for life, or at least the length of time you figure they are beneficial.

Determining the most beneficial habits

Determining the good habits to initiate that will benefit you most is easiest when taking a complete assessment of your current bad habits. It gives you a cheat sheet that allows you to see the areas in your life that are in need of a little reorganization or attention to specific details. You probably already have somewhat of an incomplete mental list already. Choosing from there will depend on how you highlight them in order of importance. Overwhelming yourself with changes will not be helpful and could actually make you give up in a short amount of time.

Focus on Learning Instead of Past Failure

If you try and focus on failure, your mind will gravitate towards it every time. Many of the most powerful men and women in business have had to file bankruptcy and create a business more than once. Rather than looking at it as a failure, they chose to view it in the light of education and learning. Failure is a negative term that leaves no room for actual improvement of skill, knowledge, and business acumen. Giving an idea a try and learning from a few mistakes is putting it to a brighter and more positive level.

Chapter 12. Why Negative Emotions Can Fuel Your Success

However positive you are and however well you may set yourself up for success, there will be times of despair, sadness, anger, and frustration. To be human is to experience a full spectrum of emotions. Most of us try and shy away from any kind of negative feelings. When we feel bad, we often try to forget about it as soon as possible and get back to feeling happy or at least "OK" as quickly as possible. I'm going to argue that not only is it healthy to embrace your negative emotions, but that they are great fuel when it comes to self-control and bolstering your sense of purpose.

As long as you have come to accept that suffering is inevitable, you are ready to make good use of your unpleasant emotions. Negative feelings like sadness or despair are clear signals that something is wrong and needs to change. Think your negative emotions not as an inconvenience that needs to be "solved," but rather as helpful signposts that highlight what steps you must take in order to improve your quality of life.

134

Instead of harnessing their negative emotions in a constructive manner, using them as an incentive to put together a plan of action, most people try and ignore uncomfortable feelings. They hope that somehow the problem will resolve itself! We're back again to a central theme of this book – you won't make any solid progress until you back up your thoughts and analysis with concrete action! Let's look at a few specific negative emotions and how you can best channel them. Humans are emotion-driven creatures who gravitate towards drama, so you may as well make the most of your negative energy.

We'll start by taking a fresh look at anger and rage. Lots of us have trouble dealing with these feelings, and much of the trouble comes from how we are socialized. We may have been taught from a young age that it's "not nice" to get angry, and that if we allow ourselves to get angry then we'll spiral out of control. As a result, we suppress even our justifiable rage and seethe with frustration. On the other hand, some of us are taught that anger is a good way to get other people to do what you want. If you live by this rule, you will end up in lots of heated confrontations. Obviously, neither approach is particularly healthy.

Instead, aim to use the physical charge of anger as an energy supply. This could be as simple as channeling your energy into a hard workout at the gym. However, it can also be a great motivator that pushes you towards long term goals. For example, you may be angry at your peers in high school or college for saying or implying that you are fat, stupid, or ugly. You might be able to rise above their comments, but why not use your rage as a basis for positive change? It isn't healthy to base your life decisions on what other people say or do, but it can certainly propel you forwards. A desire to prove once and for all that you are not useless, that you can do and be whatever you like and triumph over whatever obstacles life places in your way can give you a much-needed boost when you feel like giving up.

Envy is another powerful negative emotion that you can put to excellent use. When you feel envious, this is a clue that someone else has exactly what you want. This is actually a gift, because it helps you discover precisely what you need to work on. If you catch yourself envying someone else's material possessions, this is a sign that you might want to build up your own wealth. This provides you with a solid starting point for putting together a blueprint for greater financial freedom and security. Look closely at your feelings of envy, write out what it is you want, and during those times when you want to give up return to your list.

What about anxiety? Believe it or not, your tendency to worry can actually work in your favor. Fear can be immobilizing but used properly it can be the first step towards great success. This can work in two ways. First, conquering your fears is satisfying in and of itself, so imagining how good you will feel when you have done something that scares you is a powerful motivator. Second, you can use fear as a basis for constructive action. For example, let's say that the company you work for is in financial trouble, and your job is at risk. This may be just the push you need to think about applying for a better job, starting your own business, or retraining for a new career. Fear can be managed but rarely obliterated, so you may as well make the most of it!

If you feel overwhelmed by anxiety, sit down and make a list of how you could handle the outcomes you fear most. Assuming that the worst were to happen, how could you make the best of a bad situation? For example, you may be afraid to rent out your house, quit your job and travel the world for a year even though it's one of your most beloved ambitions.

Identify what it is that actually frightens you. In this example, you may be afraid that you will be unemployable when you return home. The next step is to think of realistic solutions you could use if your worst fears actually came true. To continue with the above instance, you could retrain for a new career or find an entry-level job in a new sector and spend a couple of years working your way back into better-paying positions. This exercise proves that fear can be a trigger for creative thinking and problem-solving.

Too many people assume that if they are afraid, they are going in the wrong direction. Fear doesn't work like that – in fact, if the thought of making a change or heading in a new direction scares you, it's a positive sign! It means that you are heading out of your comfort zone, which is a necessary condition for progress. Think back to those times in your life when you had to push yourself through a major challenge. You probably felt a strong sense of fear at times, because you were stepping into the unknown. Never let fear hold you back, and don't fight against it. Accept it as a natural human response and focus on moving towards your goal step by step. Everyone feels afraid from time to time. The difference between successful and unsuccessful people is that the former press on anyway and allow their fears to keep them focused on their goals, whereas the latter allow themselves to overthink their situation and become paralyzed.

Despair and sadness are harder to channel into success, but with a bit of imagination they can be a wonderful foundation for self-discipline and achievement. For example, let's say that you have recently gone through a difficult divorce and also lost one of your best friends in the space of a few months. These kinds of events can seriously deplete your focus unless handled properly. A good first step is to remind yourself that everything changes, and that you won't feel like this forever. When we experience a significant loss, it often triggers a period of intense self-reflection. When you learn the ability to discern what is actually vital to a good life from what is unnecessary, your focus and time management skills will greatly improve. The "big things" like following your dreams and pursuing goals suddenly come into focus, and trivial activities such as watching TV or gossiping about other people start to fade into the background. You begin to channel your efforts into achieving something worthwhile rather than merely passing time. Self-discipline becomes easier because you get into the habit of paying attention to what is actually going to help you achieve your aims.

Have you ever read an inspiring story about someone who achieved a big goal in memory of a friend or relative? Some people find that the worst moments in their lives, such as losing a partner to an illness, can prompt them to succeed in ways they could never have imagined. A common example are people who go from being couch potatoes to marathon runners in order to raise money for a relevant charity. These runners often start out with no athletic interests whatsoever, but the knowledge that they are raising money and awareness in someone's memory means that they reorder their priorities. You may also have read about people who become full-time campaigners following horrific events that have taken place in their lives. These examples are proof that negative feelings can be harnessed in a positive manner.

If your goals are creative in nature – for example, you want to write a novel or become a better artist – you'll be encouraged to know that research demonstrates how negativity can help you! Researchers from Ghent University tracked the daily habits and emotions of 102 full-time creative professionals. They discovered that the participants were most productive on days in which they woke up in a bad mood. This suggests that negative feelings can be directly transformed into creative output.

Why not immerse yourself in art, music, writing or other similar activity when you next feel angry or sad?

Shame is another unpleasant emotion that holds many of us back from engaging with the world and going after what we want. Note that shame isn't the same as guilt. Guilt is a normal, healthy sensation of having done wrong. Shame, however, is deeper and damages a person's sense of self. When you feel shame, you are in effect telling yourself "I am a bad person." It's hard to put in the work needed to move forward when you have no sense of self-worth. After all, if you think you are fundamentally flawed, you won't feel that you even deserve to make your life better. The good news is that you can deal with shame and develop a healthier attitude.

In her book Daring Greatly, author Brene Brown outlines exactly how we can do this. The first step is to open up to someone else about our feelings, because once we gain a sense of acceptance from someone else, we are more likely to forgive ourselves. Ask a non-judgmental friend to listen to you as you process guilt and shame or consider seeing a professional counselor if this is a major problem for you.

There is no need to carry shame around with you – it doesn't help anyone, and it certainly won't help you develop self-discipline. Brown explains that in letting go of shame we grow in compassion, both for ourselves and others. This entails accepting that everyone is human, everyone makes mistakes, and everyone deserves the chance to move on and start again. Remember how we talked about failure earlier on in this book, and established that dwelling on past mistakes drains you of the energy and drive you need to succeed in the present? Conquering shame is an essential step if you want to de-clutter your mind and focus on what you want most. Whatever you may have done in the past, you still deserve a positive self-image and the chance of success. Choose to see feelings of shame as a valuable opportunity to take on a more realistic view of the world and drop the habit of berating yourself.

Chapter 13. Improving Focus And Concentration

Another important characteristic of the Spartans and Special Operations Units is their ability to focus no matter where they are and what they are doing. Most of their missions require high concentration and focus. The opposite can prove dangerous and fatal. Snipers have to focus on their target if they want a sure hit.

Soldiers have to be alert at all times during combat to know if enemies are coming. People who are scatterbrained and who always find themselves daydreaming have no room in such kinds of missions. They will just put them, and their team's lives in danger and also jeopardize the operation. This can cost a lot of time, resources, and life.

Some people think that the most difficult part of a sniper's job is to successfully shoot the target from afar but there's a lot more to a sniper's job than this. In fact, what's even more difficult for them is to go to a dangerous area, like the enemy's lair, to collect reconnaissance, and be as invisible and silent as possible.

Being seen or heard by the enemy is fatal, which makes it a lot more difficult than simply sitting somewhere far from the target and trying to find the right angle to shoot. Being invisible and silent is extremely difficult especially if you are a hulking man carrying gears and equipment. Add the fact that you also feel hungry, thirsty, tired, and sleepy, every aching muscle and bone in your body screaming for rest. It is easy to lose focus with all these distractions and challenges, but a great soldier never loses focus and keeps moving until he completes his task.

Your challenges in life may not be a matter of life or death but you can apply the same techniques that these elite soldiers are using to improve their mental focus and concentration.

What is focus?

First, you need to know what focus means. It is the act of concentrating all your attention on something, whether it is an object, an activity, a task, an event, and so on. The definition may seem boring to you but there is more to focus than simply concentrating on one thing. More often than not, several different things sometimes try to get your attention, and this is what makes you lose focus on what you are doing. So aside from concentrating on one thing, focusing is also the act of ignoring other things, which sounds easier said than done.

Eliminating other factors that will divide your attention is an important prerequisite of focus. You have to say yes to only one thing, and no to the rest so that one thing will have your full and undivided attention. Saying no to those other things is not permanent. It is just saying no to doing those things at that particular instant. To be productive, you need to have focus. Focus on the things that matter and eliminate the distractions. You also have to prioritize the things that you need to focus on.

Here are some steps that you can try to improve your focus.

Stop, look, listen, and smell

When you find yourself distracted from fatigue, hunger, and the difficulty of your task, you need to shift your focus and attention from your mission and try to take a short break by doing SLLS. You should stop what you are doing at the moment, look all around you, listen to any small movement, and smell your surroundings. The main objective of taking an SLLS break is to refocus and also take a much-needed break, albeit a short one. This will at least keep you mindful of your surroundings and will help you focus on your mission.

This is also helpful in an office setting when you find yourself bombarded by emails that you feel you should respond to right away and the hundred and one tasks that your boss wants you to do. Try to refocus by doing SLLS. This is especially helpful if you have a lot of things in mind and a lot of tasks to finish within the same deadline. It will help keep your mind focused on what needs to be done instead of it jumping from one external stimulus to another, such as your coworker's ringing phone, the pinging of your email notification, the smell of someone's lunch heating in the microwave, the high pile of papers on your desk, and many other things that can get you distracted.

Stop whatever it is you are doing, look around you and try to organize the piles of paper on your desk, listen to the ringing phone of your coworker until he picks it up, and simply enjoy the smell of the food. Sometimes, all you need is to be mindful of the things around you instead of simply reacting to them impulsively and negatively. Just take it all in especially if there is really nothing you can do about them. Just make them a part of your groove.

Situational awareness

The Special Forces Units are taught a technique called situational awareness. It is defined as the ability to understand important factors and elements of the current situation of the troop in relation to their mission. In short, being aware of your surroundings and what's happening around you.

During combat, situational awareness is crucial because it can help you save lives. People today are not often aware of their surroundings. When you go to the airport or a shopping mall, do you think these people are aware of their surroundings?

Probably not. They just go about their lives, inside their little bubble, not caring about what's going on around them.

You can improve your focus by doing these situational awareness exercises. This is more effective if you do it in a large, crowded place, like the mall, airport, stadium, or any place where people seem to just not care about their surroundings. These exercises will help boost your concentration and focus.

• Take note of the things that the people around you are doing

• Try to guess what they are thinking and why they are in that place

• Look for behaviors, actions, or things that you find odd or out of place

Doing these exercises will help improve your focus and will also make you pay closer attention to small details. This is something that you can use wherever you are to be able to successfully achieve your goals.

Breathe properly

Another technique that you can do to keep your focus is to learn how to breathe properly for relieving stress and tension. When you have so much stuff to do and you feel overwhelmed by it all, you should do take deep breaths to gather your wits and stay focused. When you feel your body becoming taut and tight and you notice that your breaths are faster and shallower, you are under a lot of stress and tension so try to release it by breathing properly.

By taking control of your breathing, you feel calmer and more relaxed. Start by sitting up straight with your shoulders relaxed and your hands on your lap. Empty your lungs by exhaling deeply. Fill your lungs by inhaling slowly and deeply. Count to four as you take a deep breath. Hold your breath for four seconds, then exhale slowly again for four seconds. Repeat the whole process ten times. Be sure to inhale through your nose and exhale through your mouth.

Different Special Forces Units use this technique to stay calm and focused and they call it the four-box breathing technique. The situations they are in are a lot more stressful than ordinary people usually face on a daily basis, but it works for them, which means that it will definitely work for you.

As you slowly inhale and exhale, make sure that all your muscles are relaxed, especially your tongue, jaw, and forehead. You probably don't notice it but when you feel stressed and therefore out of focus, your forehead is wrinkled, your jaw is tight, and your tongue is stuck to the roof of your mouth. Just breathe deeply and feel all your muscles relax. You can also wiggle your toes or bend your knees a bit to further keep your body relaxed.

Have a distraction to-do list

Oftentimes, you find yourself thinking about something else while you are working on something. For example, you are finishing a report about your company's monthly sales. And sometimes, things just pop in your head, whether they are related to what you are working on or not. It is easy to fall into the trap of googling the question right so that you will have the answer right away, but this will steer you away from what you are doing.

What you can do instead is to create a distraction to-do list where you can write down all the things that crossed your mind while working and then research about them later after you finish your tasks. Questions like, "what will be the weather tomorrow", "who's that actor who starred in that movie I watched last night", "what is the title of that song", and so on. Write all of these down and get back to them later when you have free time. But first, finish your task at hand.

Meditate

Meditation does not only make you feel calm and collected and help you keep your cool in stressful situations. It also helps increase your attention span which in turn improve your focus. The longer your attention span, the longer you will be able to focus on your tasks. You do not need to spend all day meditating like monks in a monastery. You can try simple meditation techniques such as the breathing technique mentioned earlier and other tricks that can help improve your focus. This will only take a few minutes every day and you do not even need a special place to do it.

Control the voice in your head

Sometimes, the distractions are all in your head. You hear that small voice in your head that gives criticisms or distracts you from finishing your tasks. Try to control this voice and do not let it ruin your momentum, especially if it is trying to bring you down and make you feel bad about yourself or if it is trying to distract you from your task. Try to ignore this voice especially when you find yourself second-guessing your decisions and actions. If you find yourself in this predicament, just pay attention to what you are doing and try to focus on the rewards if you finish your task on time.

Another thing that you can do is to go over every little detail and every angle of your decision or task and try to find loopholes that will make it easier for that inner critic to plant seeds of doubts in your head. By understanding what needs to be done and what actions you can take in different scenarios, you will have a strong defense against your inner critic because you know what you are doing.

Focus on one thing at a time

Nowadays, companies sing the praises of people who are efficient multitaskers. In fact, it is included in the list of traits that they are looking for in their job applicants when they post job vacancies. But is multitasking really better than focusing on one single thing? The answer is that multitasking is better used in mundane tasks or tasks that do not involve deep thinking, such as talking on the phone, replying to a regular email, and printing a document. Things like these do not require you to think.

However, when it comes to finishing a task that requires your full attention, you need to focus on it alone without doing ten other different things at the same time. For example, finishing that novel that you started, creating a design for your company's website, learning how to play the piano, and so on. If you want to master any skill, you need to give it your 100% undivided attention while you are doing it.

Moreover, multitasking can lead to more mistakes than doing one task at a time because your attention is divided. To illustrate this more clearly, imagine your attention as a spotlight. If the spotlight is focused on one spot only, without moving, then you will clearly see all the details in that area. You can give more details and your description is more accurate. But if you have to move the spotlight several times in different areas, you will only catch a short glimpse of each area. Your descriptions of each area will not be as detailed and accurate because your time and resources are divided into different things.

So be sure to use your attention wisely and try to use it on things that really matter.

Practice pre-commitment

Pre-commitment is a fancier word for your to-do list. This is the act of deciding in advance what project you are going to finish first before you start working on the others and for how long you are going to work on that project. This will help you to focus more on one task because you know what needs to be done and you have a deadline for yourself.

For example, if it is a weekend, you can start working on a difficult task first, such as working out for a full hour. You can then tackle other easier tasks such as decluttering, cleaning the house, doing the laundry, washing the dishes, and so on. You can probably schedule your whole Saturday doing house chores after you finish working out so that these tasks are already out of the way and you can spend your whole Sunday just relaxing or hanging out with your family or friends. Setting a deadline for each task will also keep you from dawdling on one task and just concentrate on finishing it before the deadline.

Pay attention to the process

More often than not, people pay more attention to the end result and just pay little attention to the process. Success is not a one-time event because it involves a lot of processes along the way. It is not just a single event of losing 20 pounds in six months, getting your novel published, or achieving your target sales. It also involves your commitment to the whole process or journey of achieving that result. People who are successful in what they do fall in love with the process and the positive result is the icing on top.

For example, to become a published writer, your main goal is to get published of course but you have to fall in love with the tedious process of writing and editing and researching if you want to achieve your goal. If your goal is to lose weight, you have to fall in love with keeping in shape by eating healthy food and going to the gym. Success and rewards are just the tips of the iceberg and this is what people often see. They fail to realize that there is a lot more underneath, which includes perseverance, hard-work, discipline, and many other things that contribute to a person's success.

Chapter 14. The Universal Rules of Self-Discipline

Aside from business, sales, and finances, there are many other areas of your life that can benefit from you being more self-disciplined. In fact, every area of your life can benefit from you, focusing on this skill set, especially if you begin to follow the universal rules of self-discipline. These universal rules can be applied to virtually any area of your life and, as you do, you will discover that you begin to thrive even more in each area of your life. As you thrive more, these areas of your life will become far more enjoyable and you will find yourself experiencing a greater amount of fulfillment out of them.

These six areas, including health, relationships, romance, the relationship you share with yourself, hobbies, and faith, can all benefit from you investing in your self-discipline. Increasing your self-discipline ensures that you are always creating your most aligned vision for each area of your life and then living up to that vision, ultimately allowing you to start living the life you have always dreamt of.

The Universal Rules of Self-Discipline

The universal rules of self-discipline are, well, universal. They are going to support you in creating self-discipline in every area of your life, so I strongly recommend you take them seriously and begin to put an honest effort into making these universal rules a part of your everyday life. Even when you face a situation where being self-disciplined seems pointless, engage in self-discipline anyway. Your self-discipline is like a muscle, and the more you use it, even in seemingly pointless situations, the stronger it gets and the easier it is for you to use self-discipline in other areas of your life. Keep practicing every day and you will see yourself making huge progress toward the things that matter in your life, in every area of your life.

Start with Manageable Targets

Far too many people develop an idea of what it is that they want to achieve and then fail to think within the realms of reality. Early on, when you start toward a new goal, you find yourself feeling extremely excited about that goal and experiencing a high amount of momentum toward achieving that goal as a result of your excitement. That momentum can lead you to believe that you can achieve massive amounts of progress in short amounts of time and, if you could harness that momentum and focus entirely on that one goal, that might be true. However, most of us lose momentum over time unless we know how to harness the momentum and actually use it in our favor. The best way to harness it and work together with your natural levels of momentum is to start small and be realistic with your early targets. In fact, as you grow continue to be realistic by basing your new targets off of the ones you have already achieved, allowing you to set reasonable expectations on yourself.

Believing that you are going to be able to achieve massive targets in minimal timing is not only unrealistic, but it is completely counterproductive to your goal. In setting unrealistic targets, you intimidate yourself and ultimately encourage yourself to procrastinate or give up long before you ever begin to see any results. Sure, it may seem exciting to "go big or go home," but the truth is that is not wise, and it will not get you any results.

Rather than overwhelming yourself and then ultimately letting yourself down, develop the self-discipline of starting small. Be realistic with yourself, get to know yourself, and set up targets that you know you can reasonably work toward achieving in your life. The more you can do this, the more success you will experience when it comes to achieving goals in your life.

Be Honest About What You Want

Believe it or not, a lot of people are still living out their lives trying to meet other people's expectations and trying to achieve the dreams that other people have for them. There is a saying in the business world that goes, "If you don't work toward your dream, someone else will employ you to work toward theirs." This is true in far more areas of your life than just the business world, and if you are not careful, you could find yourself chasing all of the wrong dreams your entire life. When you chase the wrong dreams, which are essentially just someone else's dream for you, what you end up doing is working toward things that you genuinely do not care about. As a result, you find yourself feeling passive toward your goals and procrastinating rather than getting them done which, in the end, only feeds a lack of self-discipline rather than the creation of self-discipline.

When it comes to being more disciplined, you need to make sure that what you are working toward aligns with what you actually care about in your life. You need to be moving toward your own dreams, and you need to be clear on what those dreams look like and how they are different from the life you are already living. As you cultivate your own dream and work toward that, get specific on how you can change your current approach to life to help you start living life your way. The more clear you can be about what it is that you want to change, the easier it will be for you to actually make and commit to these changes so that you can see the results you desire.

As you begin to work toward your personal dreams, make sure you are also being disciplined in that you are making choices that fit your needs and desires. In other words, if it is your dream to become healthier and someone else has told you the only way to do that is to drink kale smoothies, but you hate kale, ditch the kale. Go with something else that is going to be healthier and more in alignment with something you enjoy so that you are both working toward what it is that you desire and enjoying the process of getting there.

Take Control of the Situation

Far too often, people forget that they are in control over their own lives and that it is their responsibility to make sure that the life they are living aligns with the life that they actually want to be living. In fact, this happens so often that many people fail to realize they are even doing this which results in them sitting around waiting for someone to hand them opportunities and results because they forget that this is their responsibility. If you want to increase your self-discipline, you need to remember that you are the adult of the situation and that you are solely responsible for your own life and for the results you see inside of your own life. Spending your life waiting for someone else to bring you those results will only lead to you receiving a lot of nothing because no one is coming to your rescue. No one is capable of giving you the results you desire even if they wanted to because, to put it simply, you can choose to ignore them.

Rather than sitting around waiting for the results to fall in your lap, realize that this is never going to happen and that you have to go out there and get what you want for yourself. Don't sit around and wait for someone to tell you to get into action, and don't blame everyone else for why things are not getting done in your life because the only person responsible for your results is you. You may need to give up on some of your down time, make compromises, or sacrifice a few things to get where you want to go, but once you start seeing the results you desire, you will realize that it is well worth the effort.

If you find that you are really struggling to give yourself permission to do things your way and to enjoy life your way, you may need to start small and work up to the point that you want to be at. No matter how small you have to start, though, the goal is to start and get moving. Over time you will grow used to the fact that you are the one in charge and making decisions to move your life forward will come a lot easier for you, allowing you to make continued progress toward your personal goals.

Stay as Organized As Possible

Organization is an essential part of self-discipline. Getting organized in and of itself is a discipline as most people find that it is easier to stay disorganized since it requires virtually no effort to live a messy life. Well, at least, not on the surface. The truth is, however, if you are living a messy life, you are going to end up putting a lot more effort in later on because you have to work through the mess to get to what you need. Plus, mess and disorganization has been proven to reduce mental wellness and increase stress which means that every time you choose to live a disorganized life, you are also choosing to increase the resistance you feel toward everything you do.

Getting organized requires you to actually get physically organized by taking care of your surroundings, as well as get organized by cleaning up your schedule and maintaining your to do list. The more you can keep your entire life organized, the better you are going to feel, and the less resistance you will experience toward the various things in your life.

Start this discipline by cleaning your house, car, office, and any other area that you spend a lot of time in that you are able to clean up. Eliminate clutter, get rid of garbage, and make sure

164

that everything in that space has its own place so that you no longer have any excuses as to why your belongings are so messy. Once you have completely cleaned the space, you need to start focusing on the discipline of keeping it clean by putting everything back when you are doing using it and spending 5-15 minutes per day maintaining that space. The better you can do this, the better you are going to feel, and the easier your life is going to be.

For your schedule, you are going to do the same thing. Start by cleaning up your calendar and your to do list. Eliminate things that are irrelevant or that do not matter, and delegate wherever you can if you find that your schedule or to do list is overwhelming and contains more than you can reasonably handle. After you have effectively tidied up your schedule, you need to keep it that way by making sure that everything gets placed onto your schedule or to do list, and by making sure that everything that does get placed on there is important. Stop committing to tasks you cannot handle, say no when you are overbooked, and make sure that you continue to offer yourself plenty of time to get things done. The better you can take care of your schedule, the better you will feel.

Make Choices Ahead of Time

Sometimes, it can be easy to go back on your discipline if you find yourself in a "grey area." For example, let's say you have a goal that you want to spend more quality time with your loved ones, and while you are at a loved one's house, they become busy doing something, such as looking for something or tidying up. If you have not yet made the decision, it might be easy to choose to get out your phone and start texting or scrolling social media while that person takes care of whatever it is that they are doing. However, doing this only means that you are taking away from your focus and attention by distracting yourself with your phone. Still, you may be able to justify it to yourself because that person is busy for the moment and so it should not interrupt the quality of your time spent together. When you justify this, because you never made a decision in the first place, you may find yourself later regretting the decision you made. For example, maybe while you checked your phone, you saw something that was interesting or important, and now you are distracted by that topic. Rather than being able to focus on being present with your loved one, you find yourself continually thinking about what you read and feeling impatient to respond or take care of said thing.

These types of situations can come up in many ways in your life. If you do not decide what you are going to do in advance, you might find yourself betraying your diet at a restaurant or ditching your exercise routine on vacation. You might find that you engage in activities that distract you from your hobbies, that prevent you from fully immersing yourself into your faith, or that hold you back from making progress toward building a relationship with yourself. Anytime something unexpected comes up, you may make a poor decision that ultimately leads to you not fulfilling what it was that you wanted to fulfill, only to realize what you have done at a later date.

Instead of throwing yourself into unexpected situations and making poor decisions, resolve to make choices ahead of time. Create plans for what you are going to do should unexpected situations arise and work toward putting those plans in motion any time an unexpected situation actually does come up. The more you can stay on track with making these plans for unexpected moments and following them through, the better you will be at staying on track with your self-discipline.

Take Advantage of Technology

Technology is an inevitable part of our lives and, whether you want to admit it or not, it likely plays a huge role in your life as well. One study showed that the average person spends 3 hours 15 minutes on their phone per day, with more avid users spending more than four and a half hours on their devices per day. With how connected we are and how often we find ourselves relying on our phones, it is important to realize that technology is not something we can fight against. Instead, you should focus on having two disciplines around technology, with the first being that you will use it as little as possible. Rather than spending hours every single day plugged in and connected to technology, consider unplugging and finding other things to do, such as picking up a hobby or investing in relationships that you care about. Being disciplined in spending your time doing more things than just filling the hours with social media is a powerful opportunity to spend your life doing things that matter more than just sitting around, wasting your time.

When you are using technology, practice working with it to benefit your life rather than letting it overrule your life. Have boundaries on how often you will use your phone and on how you will use your phone when you do use it. If you need to use the screen time application and commit to letting the screen limit prevent you from opening and using any of your applications, such as social media. You can use applications like your timer and alarm to help schedule your day, as well as download applications like a mobile scheduling program to help you stay organized and keep yourself on track. Using these different features will make staying disciplined with your device a lot easier.

Everyone Gets Tempted

It is human nature to get tempted by things, especially when we know that those things will bring us instant gratification. We want to feel fulfilled and good in every moment, which is why engaging in things like self-discipline is so challenging in the first place since, in most cases, self-discipline, includes delaying gratification. However, learning how to delay your gratification is crucial if you want to engage in self-discipline as delayed gratification ensures that you can focus more intently on getting important things done rather than wasting your time engaging in meaningless temptations.

I would like to discuss two additional practices you might consider trying to help you get through temptations more effectively. The first thing you should try includes creating a distraction box. A distraction box is a small box that you keep nearby whenever you are doing anything, and anytime you find yourself being distracted by something, you put it in the box. Putting distractions such as your phone, the office stapler, fidget spinners, and other things that get you distracted in the box means you are less likely to touch them and more likely to focus on the task at hand. Commit to not grabbing anything out of the box unless absolutely necessary until you are completely finished with the task you want to be working on.

Conclusion

You have made it to the end of this book, and that is commendable. I am certain that your knowledge of self-discipline has been increased many times fold. It may surprise you that one of the main reasons why people lack self-discipline is the lack of knowledge in the first place. Some don't know that self-discipline can be built. Others don't know how to build it.

We often admire people who are disciplined. Those that always manage to do what needs to be done. After going through this book, you now know that self-discipline is not inborn. It is a habit that can be created and cultivated. That means that you can achieve self-discipline, which allows you to reach for your goals one step at a time.

Have you identified mistakes that you have been making in your quest for success? One of the most common ones is the misconception that you always have to feel motivated in order to take action. You look at the people around you are accomplishing things, and you imagine that they always wake up with the urge to get things done.

This could not be further from the truth. Even the high achievers have days when they don't want to get out of bed, just like you do. What separates them from the rest is that they do it anyway. With that in mind, you don't have to wait a day longer to kick off your action plan.

Have you tried before and failed? I'm sure you have now changed your mindset about failure. You will no longer have to cringe about the setback that you suffered. Failure is not meant to be fatal. You can leverage on defeat and bounce back even stronger.

Having gone through the book now is the time to plan. Get your goals right, then develop an action plan. Break the main goal into smaller goals that you can attend to daily. You can include an accountability partner to keep you in check.

This is not one of those books that you read once and tuck away. This you keep close, so you can refer to it every so often. Feel free to recommend it to your peers, so that they too can develop their self-discipline and attain the highest possible level of success.

The path to excellent self-discipline is a long and winding journey. Young men who wish to become Navy SEALs don't simply show up one day and have that honor bestowed upon them. They have to work incredibly hard for that title, and it is only given when they have proven beyond a shadow of a doubt that they have what it take both physically and mentally to get the job done.

As you pursue your own goals and dreams, remember to keep the model of the SEALs in mind. This book has created an outline for you to follow in terms of the processes and traits required to become the self-disciplined person that you desire to be.

CPSIA information can be obtained
at www.ICGtesting.com
Printed in the USA
LVHW080154201220
674638LV00005B/86